THE 40:40 PRINCIPLE

MENTORING

YOUR ROAD MAP TO FINDING LIFE-CHANGING MENTORS

ANDY CHRISTIANSEN

WESTBOW
PRESS®
A DIVISION OF THOMAS NELSON
& ZONDERVAN

Artwork by Misenheimer Creative, Inc.
www.misenheimer.com

WestBow Press books may be ordered through booksellers or by contacting:

WestBow Press
A Division of Thomas Nelson & Zondervan
1663 Liberty Drive
Bloomington, IN 47403
www.westbowpress.com
844-714-3454

ISBN: 978-1-4497-0071-3 (sc)
ISBN: 978-1-4497-0072-0 (hc)
ISBN: 978-1-4497-0070-6 (e)

Library of Congress Control Number: 2010923050

Print information available on the last page.

WestBow Press rev. date: 01/04/2023

To Drew, Cole, and Mati,
the next generation of mentoring with the 40:40 Principle.

Contents

Acknowledgments

This book is a compilation of hundreds of relationships, involving thousands of conversations over dozens of years. It began as an idea at age fifteen and grew into a lifestyle twenty-five years later. This book would not have happened without my uncle, Frank B. "Buck" Carr, who coined the principle. The biggest influence on my life and this book came from his mother, my maternal grandmother, Anita B. Carr. She stepped in to be my mother figure during my formative years, when my biological mother was inactive and often absent. My grandmother taught me the power of focus, the love of being a lifetime learner, and the joy of serving others and the community as a volunteer.

People told me that writing a book is like having a baby. Well, I don't know about that, but I have witnessed a few births. I will say that writing *The 40:40 Principle* was exhilarating to my spirit but exhausting to my patience. It was like mowing the lawn with scissors! The main people who helped improve my patience and this book were Don Sadler, Major Blake Peirce, Kyle Lollis, Josh Bruce, and Kyle Sudu for brainstorming or editing; Misenheimer Creative for the book cover and graphics; and Reid Childers for photo and image effects.

My fifteen years in the corporate world helped shape this book. I learned early in my career that training was critical, and E. & J. Gallo Winery was one of the best training companies in the consumer goods industry. Thank you, Dan Plunkett and Greg Brown, for building a Gallo dream team in Los Angeles. The sales and management training—corporate boot camp, as we called it—made an indelible mark on my life and attributed to my success. To Ron Orgiefsky, who taught me the concept of having a champion of your cause. Later, at Veryfine Products in Boston (now owned by Sunny Delight), I learned the power of innovation from then President and Owner Sam Rouse and Vice President of Sales and Marketing Bob Littlefield. Because of their confidence and support, I was able to conceptualize and brand two products: Fresh Pressed Select Harvest Veryfine Apple Juice and no-calorie, fruit-flavored spring water Fruit2O. The latter became a national brand, is now in its eleventh year of successful distribution, and has spurred a thirty-four-billion-dollar category. At Cott Beverages, Inc., Joni Huffman modeled for me the way to work with heavy hitters like 7-Eleven (Southland Corporation) and to successfully run a fifty-million-dollar business.

For modeling passion, Darrell Jones, founder of Stirred-up Ministries, and with his wife, Sarah, mentor young boys and girls in inner-city Atlanta. Fred Castellucci II, the CEO of Sugo Hospitality Group, has more love for food than any man I have ever met!

When I think about the individuals who have shaped my thinking and modeled the 40:40 Principle (knowingly or unknowingly), I put my father, Robert H. Christiansen Sr., at the top of the list. He is the consummate people person. Thanks for being you, Dad! And to the other thoroughbreds who effortlessly model it week in and week out, year after year, thanks to the 40:40 nation: Robby Angle, Brent Batterman, Shaun Bennett, Josh Berry, Regi Campbell, Colonel Bill DeMarco, Tim Elmore, Leslie Galloway, Barry Gercu, Larry Green, Bruce Hogarth, Walter Kinzie, Julian Krevere, Fran LaMattina, Jim Lewis, Terry Masterson, Timothy Price, Casey Sanders, Scott Scoggins, Zach Thomas, John Woodall, Sam Woods, and Dennis Worden.

Thanks to key leadership mentors: Keith Ferrazzi, Patrick Lencioni, Simon Sinek, Charlie Kim, Michael Hyatt, Tai Lopez, Andy Stanley, and Rick Warren.

And thanks to my family, who put my life into perspective. My wife and best friend, Nikki Christiansen, is arguably the kindest and most big-hearted person I've ever met.

Intro

The 40:40 Principle

Better is a guide by your side than a sage
on the stage. —Andy Christiansen

Why do some people appear to succeed more in life than others? What leads to their success? Is it luck, pedigree, education, timing, talent, or relationships? Perhaps a combination of these factors? All these variables are important, but I want to suggest that the human factor—or in other words, the relationships—is one many of us overlook and neglect.

Think back over your life. Is there someone who had a profound impact on your success? Someone who stands out in the crowd, head and shoulders above everyone else? Someone who championed your cause and invested time, money, and heart into your life in a way that changed you significantly and quite possibly permanently? Someone about whom you say, "Where would I be without you in my life?"

Two are better than one, for there is a better
return for their investment. —Solomon

When I answer this question, my thoughts immediately go back to my senior year of college and the Kent State rugby team. I was co-captain of the team, and it fell to me to hire a photographer to take the official team portrait. Little did I know this seemingly simple assignment would have such an effect on me—even planting a seed for this book.

Somehow, I got the name of a local freelance photographer, Anton Cannaday, who not only took our annual team picture but also took a personal interest in me. He was about five years older than me and acted like a big brother. If he saw me doing things that were stupid, he would get in my face. He challenged me to reject passivity and accept personal responsibility for my actions—not at all easy for a fun-loving, rugby-playing college student. I didn't realize it at the time, but I was at a critical place in my life, where the choices I made would influence who I would become.

After I graduated from college, I was working in my dad's business, and I was unhappy. Anton challenged me to follow my dreams. He asked me questions like, "If you could do anything, what would you do?" It was his faith in me that gave me the courage to move to California, which led to my first major gig with E. & J. Gallo and the beginning of a successful career in the beverage industry. Mentors like Anton help us follow through on our dreams.

Mentors simply pull out the greatness
that is already within us!

To illustrate this, see the hockey stick chart below.

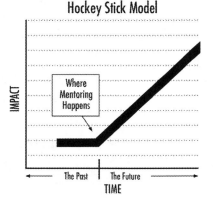

xii

Life typically takes a dramatic "upward right" trajectory when a mentor is introduced into your life. In my work as a corporate coach, I've heard many people share similar stories about people like Anton illustrating the hockey stick model. In fact, one of the questions I always ask a client is, "How did you get to where you are today?" Nearly every time, stories surface about parents, coaches, teachers, or even a sibling whose advice or guidance became a pivotal, defining moment in the client's life. Like me, the client experienced the value of mentorship, whether in a single moment or over the course of an extended relationship.

Mentoring: A relational experience where one person empowers another by sharing personal and professional resources.

My follow-up question is always, "Why don't you have someone like that in your life right now?" Despite the fact that many people have experienced the benefits of mentorship, most people *don't currently have a mentor.* There are many reasons for this lack of mentoring. Some are practical, and some are more nuanced. Once people graduate from college and stop playing organized sports, they don't have teachers and coaches who naturally fill that role. Others feel they don't have the time to develop a mentoring relationship. Another common reason is, "Why find a mentor when I can learn everything I need from conferences, podcasts, and content in its various forms found all over the Internet?" Still others express a desire to be mentored but are not sure how to get started. They feel intimidated when they think about finding the right person and asking for their time.

If any of these reasons sound familiar, then this book is for you. In the chapters to follow, we will explore how to find a mentor and begin developing a strategic relationship with them. We'll also look at the role mentors play in helping you translate knowledge into life-shaping wisdom. I'll address myths that keep us from finding a mentor, including the myth that mentors are only for the young, and that the younger generations are entitled, self-absorbed, and have unrealistic expectations that keep them from experiencing success. Nothing could be further from the truth. Everyone needs mentors, and many mentoring relationships can become a symbiotic exchange of wisdom where there is an equal amount of giving and receiving happening between the mentor and the mentee. What qualifies you to be a mentor is not age but experience, and those of us who are older have a lot to learn from the up-and-coming generation. Thus, the simplicity of the 40:40 Principle. Think of it this way: when you're in your twenties and thirties, intentionally seek out mentors over forty who can help you dream, gain confidence, and think through life-altering decisions. Then, when you're in your forties and fifties, do the same in reverse: pursue mentors under forty in order to stay socially relevant, industry knowledgeable, and physically fit. Mentors help you pinpoint ideal paths to pursue in life and work. The 40:40 Principle gives you the road map to finding life changing mentors.

I've intentionally designed this book to be compact and easy to read because I want you to spend less time in the book and more time with people. To help you get started, I've included several appendices with tools and activities to jump-start the process of finding a mentor. If you're like me and want to jump ahead, go to appendix II, "Seven Steps to Finding a Great Mentor," and get your mentoring adventure kick-started. I have also created an online video with some bonus material at www.the4040pricinple.com.

Your personal success hinges on decisions made at pivotal moments, and mentors provide the counsel you need to choose wisely. Their gift to you is masterful and invaluable; you cannot put a price on it. So break the mold, get out of your box, invest sixty minutes, and take the first step toward building a mentorship. Find the people with the experience and know-how you need, and buy them breakfast or a cup of coffee, set up a telephone meeting, or listen to something they spoke on. It just might be those sixty minutes that change everything.

Surely you need guidance to wage war, and victory
is won through many advisers. —Proverbs 24:6

Chapter 1

Mentors—Do You Need Them?

The next best thing to being wise oneself is to live
in a circle of those who are. —C. S. Lewis

When you were growing up, it's likely that several adults reached out to you. Can you recall a special relationship with a teacher, coach, or family member? Or perhaps you remember a friend's parent or youth group volunteer with a real gift for connecting with teenagers? Most of us can think of several significant people who influenced the paths we took as students. Back then, we didn't look for these advisors—they easily found us through school, sports, hobbies, and clubs.

In our early twenties, it seems like a shift takes place. No longer do mentors simply find us—we must seek them out. Who has influenced you the most since around the age of twenty-one? Take a moment to think about this question. Can you recall more than a couple of people? What changed?

My main goal in this book is to awaken and motivate you to move past isolation and the burden of figuring out life on your own. You will reap multiple benefits by tapping into the unlimited resources of *mentors*. I use the term *mentors* to describe wise individuals who possess knowledge of what is right and true and know how to successfully apply it to life—your life! In the Geography of Relationships chart from Dr. Henry Cloud below, you want to focus on people who would represent the top right quadrant (a true connection) and actively avoid those on the bottom right (the bad connection). This is what the best and the brightest people do persistently and constantly.

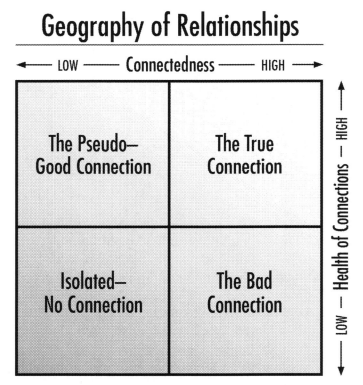

Geography of Relationships

◀— LOW —— **Connectedness** —— HIGH —▶

The Pseudo–Good Connection	**The True Connection**
Isolated–No Connection	**The Bad Connection**

LOW — **Health of Connections** — HIGH

SOURCE: HENRY CLOUD

Throughout history, famous people from all walks of life have found relationships with mentors of all ages to be one of their biggest keys to success. A vivid illustration of this principle is the interaction between three classical Greek philosophers: Socrates, Plato, and Aristotle. At the age of sixty-one, Socrates (pictured left) served as a mentor to twenty-eight-year-old Plato (pictured right). Then in like fashion, when Plato was in his sixties, he taught Aristotle, a young seventeen-year-old seeker. As you can see, wisdom travels both ways. No one is too old or too young to influence someone else.

Socrates　　　　**Plato**

The 40:40 Principle establishes a new standard for this old practice. The fact is, most people are too busy for anything more than random, casual, and topical acquaintances. As a result, many end up isolated, and they have to work longer and harder to achieve the same (or fewer) results than they could if they were tapping into a network of mentors.

> ## CONNECTING TIP #1
> *People should always come first. People over products, people over process, people over profits. People are your greatest asset!*

The Dangers of Isolation

New research suggests that loneliness or isolation can increase the risk of high blood pressure, depression, and Alzheimer's, as well as lower immunity to diseases. On the other hand, engaging in meaningful relationships appears to have the opposite effect. "Socializing appears to enhance health, and may even increase longevity," says Thomas Perls, MD, an associate professor at Boston University's School of Medicine and the founder of the New England Centenarian Study.

Our culture continues to change rapidly. Half a century ago, intentional, consistent, and challenging life-on-life relationships were built into the American fabric; they took place in the home, at work, and in the church. But times have changed. One thing that I think is needed now is more *intentionality* about these relationships. We need to make *conscious efforts* to move toward wise people and away from unwise ones.

In his book *The Principle of the Path*, Andy Stanley stresses the need for gaining wisdom from others in order to get to where you want to go in life.

> There are people who know how to get to those places (where you want to go). We know that because we've seen them there, haven't we? We know some people who have the kind of marriage we long for. We've met people whose financial house seems to be in order. You know couples with kids who are a joy to be around. Regardless of where it is you want to go, others have been there and done that. And guess what? They probably know how they got there. They have a map. And you would do well to take a peek at it if you get the opportunity.

Relationship Challenges

Much of our culture is what I call *relationally anemic*. On the outside we appear to be well-adjusted, but inwardly many of us are gripped with doubt and fear about endless things.

As the health of our relationships goes, so goes the quality of our lives. There seems to be a domino effect caused by poor relationships that leads to divorce, depression, anxiety disorders, physical maladies, job loss, and financial difficulties. Unfortunately, this trend seems to be increasing in our country rather than decreasing.

At the root of all this is an unhealthy attraction toward isolation. There are two kinds of isolation. *Overt* isolation is *direct avoidance* of people and community. You can call this conscious avoidance, as in, "I'm fully aware of how isolated I am." Meanwhile, *covert* isolation is *indirect avoidance* of people and community. This can also be referred to as subconscious avoidance and includes mental

4

and emotional avoidance: "I'm not aware of the fact that I'm doing this."

Overt isolation is easier to spot. These people are more energized by tasks than by people. They prefer to communicate by e-mail or text rather than with face-to-face interactions. They have a tendency toward being withdrawn rather than social. They would rather sit in an office with the door closed and work on tasks all day than interact with coworkers. It's not that they can't interact with people; they are simply drawn more toward tasks than socializing. They will have to work harder at creating healthy relationships and intentional conversations. However, once these people make engaging in relationships a priority, they will gain much as a result.

Covert isolation is more difficult to detect. These people are at a disadvantage because on the surface, they look like they are well connected. In fact, they are usually energized more by people than by tasks, so they are frequently around lots of other people or around at least a consistent, small group of others. The problem is that these can often be superficial relationships rather than deep ones. Even in groups and communities where relationships are supposed to go deep, they rarely do. One of the best examples of covert isolation is the local church. I have been part of more than twenty churches, including the three most influential churches in America.[1] I have seen hundreds of very "connected" people in these churches who are really in covert isolation, going through the motions of relationships without really connecting with anyone else in a deep and meaningful way.

I like to say that people who are covertly isolated (myself sometimes included) are dying of thirst while standing in two feet of water. There is so much surface relationship available that the need to go deeper seems irrelevant. You know, the five-second greeting in passing that goes, "Hey, good to see you, we need to get together sometime, gotta run to my meeting and drop off the kids at soccer practice. Call or email me. See ya." These kinds of "connections lite" are brief, topical, and empty, leaving us hungering for more depth. They're like the feeling of being hungry for solid food and eating

---

[1]   See http://www.churchrelevance.com for year 2006.

a chocolate candy bar. What happens? Your appetite subsides, but the hunger remains. The hunger pangs go away, but you're not any healthier. We need to become more intentional about developing deeper relationships: fresh fruit, vegetables, and meat and potatoes rather than junk food.

I've identified two types of covert isolation.

1. *Hollow Rabbit*—Think about the hollow chocolate bunnies you got as a kid in your Easter basket. Hollow-rabbit people (sorry to be so direct, but at least you can think of yourself as tasty) are usually busy people, but they aren't engaged. For example, there's the parent who attends her child's sporting events or school plays but is mentally checked out. Her mind is still at the office, thinking about tomorrow's meeting, or back home planning how to decorate for the holidays. This person is relationally hollow and has a difficult time being mentally present. Have you ever texted or returned emails throughout your child's entire little league game, telling yourself you're getting ahead so you can spend more time with him later? C'mon, who do you think you're kidding? Your daughter wants your undivided attention right now! The fact is when you do get home, you'll be empty, spent, and relationally wiped out.

2. *Bite-Sized Candy*—Think about individually wrapped chocolate samplers. Bite-sized candy people only offer a small portion of themselves to others. They are masters of surface dialogue, routinely keeping conversations short and sweet within their comfort zones, and only talking about things that are safe and predictable—you know, the weather, sports, or work. These people do not grow or help others grow. If you see yourself here, commit now to taking a risk, going deeper, and getting emotional with someone else.

Most of the covertly isolated people I've met fall into the category of bite-sized candy because they are always so busy, or "crazy busy" as they like to put it. To me, being busy all the time means you have given up control of your life. Or to put it more bluntly, you have lost control of the basic functionality around balancing family, work, faith, recreation, and relaxation. The question this person must ask is, "*Why* am I always so busy, and how is all this busyness benefiting me and those I love?"

My point here is that many people have lost the ability to socialize in a healthy way—to create robust relationships with wise people that will fuel their success, and to realize that they need to be intentional about converting acquaintances into friends and friends into meaningful relationships.

There are times to pull away from the crowd to maintain a healthy balance, and there are times to engage. Check yourself to ensure it's not a selfish obsession but a healthy one to steal away.

Be careful you don't overdose on vitamin "I"!

Resisting the Pull of Isolation

We are all susceptible to this pull toward isolation, whether overt or covert. In our culture today, there are countless examples of isolation's destructive potential. Personally, I have received far too many emails and phone calls from friends informing me of a suicide, illegal impropriety at work, or divorce, only to find out that these people were completely disconnected from any kind of healthy relationships. All too often they were isolated and insulated, without any outside support or encouragement.

One of the biggest problems caused by isolation is depression and anxiety. Rates of major depression have more than doubled in the United States over the past decade, according to the National Institute on Alcohol Abuse and Alcoholism. According to the World Health Organization, depression is the fourth most burdensome disease in the world, with more than 120 million people suffering from it worldwide. It's expected that by 2020, it will be the leading global disease. In the United States alone, estimates for those diagnosed with the disease range from 17–21 million people a year, or roughly 10 percent of the country. The most staggering statistic came from a leading management-consulting firm revealing: 50 percent of American workers reported on their corporate health records in 2015 that they were prescribed anxiety and depression medication, or they have reported the same as a cause for sick leave.

The first step WHO recommends for those seeking to overcome anxiety and depression is to cultivate supportive relationships with friends and family. Getting support from others plays a big role in lifting the fog of depression and keeping it away. On your own, it can be difficult to maintain perspective and sustain the effort required to beat depression. But the very nature of the illness makes it difficult to reach out for help. However, isolation and loneliness make depression even worse, so it becomes a self-fulfilling cycle.[2] It has also been my experience that the addition of medication has rescued many individuals from the deep spiral of anxiety and depression.

10 Tips for Reaching Out and Overcoming Depression/Anxiety

1. Talk to another person about your feelings
2. Help someone else by volunteering
3. Have lunch of coffee with a friend
4. Ask a loved one to regularly check in with you
5. Go to a movie, concert or small get together with someone
6. Reach out to an old friend
7. Go for a walk or a workout with a friend
8. Schedule a weekly lunch or dinner date
9. Meet new people by taking a class or joining a club
10. Confide in a counselor, therapist or clergy member

In his book *The Power of the Other,* Henry Cloud describes how others have a tremendous influence over us, whether positive or negative. Popular wisdom suggests that we should not allow

---

[2]   For tips on overcoming depression, visit http://helpguide.org/mental/depression_tips.htm.

others to have power over us, but the reality is that they do, for better or for worse. Consider the boss who diminishes you through cutting remarks versus one who challenges you to get better. Or a colleague who always seeks the limelight versus the one who gives you confidence to finish a difficult project. Or the spouse who is honest and supportive versus the one who resents your success.

Henry's research points out that when we interact with others, the software in our brains actually changes. It's people that cause us to grow.

You don't have a choice whether or not others have power in your life, but you can choose what kinds of relationships you want. —Henry Cloud

---

The charts below demonstrate years of life lost to disability, or YLD. In effect, YLD measures the equivalent years of healthy life lost through time spent in states of less than full health.[3] Note that depression tops the list for both men and women.

Years of Life Lost to Disability (YLD)

MALES

RANK	CAUSE	YLD MILLIONS	% OF TOTAL YLD
1	Unipolar depressive disorders	24.3	8.3
2	Alcohol use disorders	19.9	6.8
3	Hearing loss, adult onset	14.1	4.8
4	Refractive errors (sight loss)	13.8	4.7
5	Schizophrenia	8.3	2.8

FEMALES

RANK	CAUSE	YLD MILLIONS	% OF TOTAL YLD
1	Unipolar depressive disorders	41.1	13.4
2	Refractive errors (sight loss)	14.2	4.6
5	Hearing loss, adult onset	13.3	4.3
4	Cataracts	9.9	3.2
5	Osteoarthritis	9.5	3.1

---

[3] World Health Organization, Global Burden of Disease 2004.

Ten Ways to Interact

At the end of the day, there are many opportunities to interact with others to build and strengthen relationships. Which of these ten ways to interact with others do you most often employ? Which ones would you prefer?

---

10 Ways to Interact

1. Convey a causual greeting "good morning"
2. Compliment others
3. Collaborate around an idea
4. Communicate a "feeling "
5. Clarify your why behind the feeling
6. Create honest conflict around something that hurt you
7. Cultivate a relationship
8. Conjugate with more than one persons
9. Convene around a cause, rally or event
10. Commune (build community) over time

Whatever your normal tendency is toward relationships, keep refining them toward what you want them to be. Dig deeper, reach higher, and push further toward more meaningful connections, not less.

Think about It

- Who had the greatest impact on your life when you were growing up?

- Since, say, the age of twenty-one, who has influenced you the most?

- Do you identify more with overt isolation? (You're more energized by tasks than people and prefer e-mail or texting rather than face-to-face interactions.)

- Or would covert isolation better describe you? (You're "crazy busy" and appear to be well connected but avoid deeper, more emotional relationships by engaging in surface conversation.)

Chapter 2

Millennial Relationship Trends

We are a culture that relies on technology over community,
a society in which spoken and written words are cheap,
easy to come by and excessive. —Francis Chan

One of the biggest relationship trends of the early twenty-first century is the huge social media phenomenon. Seen as a passing or even dangerous fad just a few years ago, social media is becoming a major force in our world and is taking on a life of its own. In January 2009, there were more than 158 million unique visitors combined at the top four social media sites (MySpace, Facebook, Classmates, and LinkedIn), an increase of 58 percent over the previous year.[4] Twitter was the fastest growing social media site, growing at an annual rate of 664 percent. Tagged grew at a 421 percent clip, and Ning grew at 303 percent.

Beyond statistics, though, consider what I think is the primary reason behind the growth of this new communication medium: people are hungry to connect, but only with the right people—with *strategic* people. People are busier than ever, and as a result, they are less connected to meaningful relationships. Although many people over forty would argue that social media, texting, e-mail, and so

---

[4]   Neilson Online, "Top 20 Social Network Sites," *U.S. Home and Work*, December 2009.

on are shallow forms of relational interaction, they have not really modeled a better solution.

Some people would call social media a modern-day attempt to create the kind of intentional relationships we enjoyed a half-century ago. However, behind every tweet is a desire to connect with others, to engage in the give and take that results in new insights that can be leveraged for greater success and fulfillment. As good as this digital resource is, it will never deliver the relational benefits most people desire. Social media is a poor substitute for what we really need to succeed in life: strategic, intentional relationships with wise, trustworthy people—mentors.

> ## CONNECTING TIP #2
> *With any form of relationship, always ask yourself: What is my ultimate goal for my relationship with this person? To socialize and have fun? To learn something new? To invest in them relationally? To network? To build my career?*

For those who interact in the social media space, it is authentic and relevant to who they are. It provides an excellent source of data and information so that when they do connect with someone in person, they are able to hit the ground running. The tagline for relationships today may be "a mile wide and an inch deep," but I believe the younger generations are hungry for relationships that are deeper than this—for a little more *quality* and a little less quantity. They have a genuine interest in and appreciation for other people. For them, more time with fewer people equals greater life satisfaction.

Time, Money, or People?

Ironically, of the three basic resources at everyone's disposal—time, money, and people—people are most often overlooked. But they are also usually the most available resource; time and money are always limited, but people are unlimited. Don't let people be your missing link and the barrier between you and the life you know you want.

Time, Money, People

Use the graph below to identify where you think you are relationally and, most important, where you desire to be.

Isolated • **Acquainted** • **Connected**
(People are optional)   (People are all right)   (People are strategic)

Finally, keep these 3 "people goals" in mind:

1. Be *intentional* rather than random.
2. Be *focused* rather than scattered.
2. Be *purposeful* rather than pressured.

How Culture Influences Lifestyle

Let's take a brief look back at how relationship trends have developed from the middle part of the twentieth century through today's infatuation with social media.

Prior to the 1950s, mentors were fairly common. People could count on family members—moms, dads, grandparents, aunts, and uncles—to provide wisdom, challenges, and encouragement. But over the past few decades, it seems that our mentors have gotten as busy and distracted as we are. Additionally, the economic environment has all but removed training, mentoring, and modeling from the marketplace outside of the traditional annual conference, which serves more as a simple motivational event than a training opportunity.

Even broader than this, our society has changed dramatically over the past century and will most likely change even more rapidly over the next couple of decades. Ask yourself, "Am I clear on these changes and prepared to capitalize on them?" To get perspective on this and better prepare for the future, let's go back a little further.

For most of humankind's history, the world has been an agricultural society, with most people living and working on farms. As a result, relationships tended to be family-centric. This model took a dramatic shift around 1850, when the Industrial Revolution moved many people from manual-based labor to a more automated form of working. People moved from rural farms to small towns and urban city centers, and relationships spread outside the family to include the local community.

The Industrial Revolution continued to shape the world well into the late twentieth century, allowing people to move out from towns and cities into the suburbs, where many lived in subdivisions or master-planned neighborhoods. Relationships subsequently shifted away from family and community to center around the marketplace and neighbors. The Industrial Revolution also provided us with another dramatic shift, this time in consumer demand. Since the 1950s, there has been an endless stream of media promoting consumer products and services that offer the promise of a simpler life. As a result, many people have overextended their financial capacities, their time working away from home, and even their physical health.

The problem with all this is isolation. The speed of life has created lives almost void of significant human interaction or meaningful human touch. Think about it: most of us rise early in the morning and have little family or friend interaction before rushing out the door for work or school. On the way, we hit a drive-through window, where we are greeted by a well-meaning talking head, and then we pull into the gas station, where we pay at the pump. Once at work, we go to our private office or cubical, where we usually eat lunch alone (if we eat at all).

After work, we rush home while talking on the cell phone and listening to the radio, stopping at another drive-through for an evening meal. We relax for a few minutes alone because the rest of the family is working late or at a dance recital or soccer practice, ingest our ninety-nine-cent heart attack in a sack, and then turn to the source of our most consistent and reliable relationships—that gorgeous, enthralling, captivating, giant TV screen! Here we are entertained and numbed until well past bedtime, when we doze off in front of our dear friend the TV—only to wake up early the next morning to hit the replay button and go through the same routine again.

Is this the American dream that most of us grew up envisioning? Probably not. My point is simply that this kind of lifestyle and routine is preventing many of us from being more strategic with our relationships.

During the early 1990s, the industrial age began to take on more of a specialized niche identity. The trend was moving away from manufacturing things and toward the dissemination of information—electronics, speed, and portability—with an ever-increasing appetite for more. Today, we refer to this shift as the start of the information age, which includes the Internet that affects virtually every area of our lives. People can now work inside or outside of the traditional workplace; as a result, relationships have shifted from marketplace- and neighbor-centric to highly random, erratic, and superficial ones at work and at home.

We've touched briefly on the exploding popularity of social media: Twitter, Facebook, Instagram, YouTube, and all the other new electronic communities that have sprung up. This is driven primarily by Generation Y, the sixty million people born between 1977 and 1994. They are fed up with the anemic, random connections modeled by their parents' generation, the baby boomers, who built a legacy of individualism and self-fulfillment. Gen Y is screaming, "Enough already!" and is intentionally going back to the basics of human relationships that form the foundation of the 40:40 Principle. They hunger for authenticity, openness, and choice.

On the positive side, social media allows people to upload much of their lives to others online, and to download others' lives too. It creates conversations that may not otherwise exist and allows for frequency of interaction and platonic intimacy. Paradoxically, however, the very things Generation Y says they are rejecting—individualism and self-fulfillment—are what they're actually embracing, only electronically. Of course, social media is still in its infancy; so much is still to be learned about its effects on relationships.

Now, before you take a breather, absorb one more reality. Today we have moved beyond the information age to what many experts are now calling the creative age, the age of wisdom, or the knowledge worker age.[5] It is defined as a time when *people* are the asset—not the farm, the factory, or the electronic tool. This is an absolute game-changer, and much of our global economy is not prepared for it. Most of the business models today focus on old systems of management: do this, do that, or go find another job. This old, autocratic style of leadership must be replaced with a more democratic and honoring style that asks what is the best use of human capital and matches it with the work to be done to create maximum efficiency and productivity.

Why Go It Alone?

Think about it. What US president would ever enter the office saying, "I'll do it alone—no vice president, no cabinet, no advisors"? What business owner would ever try to run all aspects of her company alone: finance, sales, marketing, planning, and human resources? We would consider that individual shortsighted and unwise. Yet many people in all walks of life assume that they don't need anyone else to help them succeed, only to find themselves burned out, depressed, or frustrated with the outcome.

In a multitude of counselors there is safety. —Solomon

---

[5] Stephen R. Covey, *The 8th Habit*, chapter 1.

Would it be advantageous for you to tap into your available pool of mentors to broaden your perspective and strengthen your mental muscles to make better decisions? If you do not have an available pool of advisors, this book will tell you how to build one. Today, we are busier than ever and overloaded with information. The time you have to process decisions and opportunities is at greater risk every day, so why go it alone? In fact, if you do go it alone, you set yourself up for added pressure on your ability to succeed.

The 40:40 Principle is not just a one-way tool; it works both ways. It can serve as a road map to help align you with mentors who will keep you focused on and pointed toward long-term success. It can be a valuable tool to help you increase your effectiveness at work and at home, and it can determine your vocational calling, purpose, and destiny in life, ultimately landing you in a place of success and significance. It can help you recharge your batteries and see things from a fresh perspective through the eyes of someone *half* your age, or someone *twice* your age. It can help you determine whether you are on the right track to achieving your goals and objectives—and if not, help you shift course so that you can get on the right track.

The question you will need to ask yourself is this: "Am I more comfortable staying where I am, or would acquiring a few mentors and putting the 40:40 Principle into practice significantly enhance my ability to succeed?" The concepts that underlie the 40:40 Principle have been in the DNA of successful people from Socrates and Plato to some of today's most recognized business, entertainment, and sports superstars—people like Bono, Oprah Winfrey, Ben Roethlisberger, and Peter Drucker, all of whom have tapped into the secrets of the 40:40 Principle during their lives.

Get Ready to Stretch!

As you continue reading, prepare to be stretched in three key areas.

Relationships—These are important, because other people heavily influence us. "You are known by the company you keep," as the old saying goes. Hang out with turkeys, and you become

Thanksgiving dinner, but spend time with eagles, and you'll soar in the heavens. It is important to determine what your circle of friends looks like in relation to the success you desire in life. Ask yourself whether they are helping you succeed or holding you back.

How many friends do you currently have and meet with regularly, who both challenge and encourage you? If you can count them on more than one hand, you are relationally healthy. If you have three to five, you are relationally average. But if you only have one or two, you're barely surviving relationally. The people I know who are wildly successful in life can count these relationships past both hands. The president of the United States, for example, has fifteen cabinet members advising him, most CEOs have between six and twelve directors, and top professional athletes have at least half a dozen trainers, coaches, and agents.

2. *Attitude*—We are what we eat, nutritionists tell us, but we are also what we *think*. Like kinds attract each other, so if your attitude is healthy, you'll attract other people with healthy attitudes. Unfortunately, the opposite is true if your attitude is unhealthy. For example, think about how complainers tend to gravitate toward each other until they concoct a giant pity party.

If you continuously repeat negative statements to yourself that you can't, you're fearful, you're pessimistic, and so on, then your attitude will eventually control your actions. If, on the other hand, your attitude is one of positivity and optimism, this will lead to positive actions and outcomes. Having mentors in your life will help you turn the tide away from negative thoughts and outcomes and toward positive ones, thus setting you up for success. The more successful people you surround yourself with, the more successful you will be, and vice versa.

3. *Lifestyle*—This is defined as "a way of life or style of living that reflects the attitudes and values of a person or group." Therefore, I suggest that your lifestyle is a combination of your relationships and your attitude.

Relationships + Attitude = Lifestyle

You do the math: healthy relationships plus a healthy attitude will equal a healthy lifestyle, whereas unhealthy relationships plus an unhealthy attitude will equal an unhealthy lifestyle.

You might be wondering where money fits into all this. I believe that money will only give you an *illusion* of the ideal lifestyle. I have friends who are millionaires and friends who possess very little, and they all have roughly the same joys and sorrows. They all struggle with relationships, healthy attitudes, and mental and emotional happiness. Ultimately, a healthy lifestyle is not something you can purchase or something you should hope for. It is a by-product of intentional decisions you make regarding the people you surround yourself with and the attitude you cultivate. With this approach, you can survive and thrive regardless of your circumstances.

Think about It

- The social media phenomenon reveals that people are hungry to connect, but digital resources cannot deliver what we really want: strategic, intentional relationships with wise, trustworthy people.

- Review what a typical day looks like for you. How deep are your conversations?

- How would you describe the attitude and lifestyle of your closest friends and colleagues?

- In relation to the success you desire, are your current friends and colleagues helping you succeed or holding you back?

Chapter 3

How It Works

In this information age, we are easily the most
informed, and over-informed generation ever.
But what comes with that is being the most mis-
informed age ever too!—Andy Christiansen

It wouldn't be a stretch to say that the generation born from
1980 through 1995, with a current age in 2016 of twenty-one to
thirty-six, is the "smartest" generation to ever inhabit planet Earth,
or at least they're the most informed. For starters, they have access
to more data than ever before. For example, one edition of the *New
York Times* contains more information than the seventeenth-century
man or woman would have encountered in an entire lifetime.[6] And
amazingly, over the last thirty years, mankind has produced more
information than in the previous five thousand years.[7] But is this
really a good thing? Could it be that the sheer volume of information
is actually causing us to be *less* smart? In his book *Data Smog*, David
Shenk describes how a thing called *information overload* is slowing us
down and making it *harder*, not easier, to make important decisions.
In one study, he notes that in 1971 the average person received 560
marketing messages per day. By 1997, that number had increased

---

[6]   S. A. Wurman, *Information Anxiety* (New York: Doubleday, 1987), 32.

[7]   *Reuters Magazine,* Lexis Nexis Universe (4/28/98), "Information Overload
Causes Stress" (March–April 1997).

to more than 3,000 messages per day. Just think what that number must look like today! This also begs the question: Could we be the most *mis*-informed generation ever?[8]

It seems obvious to me that success in our knowledge-based economy requires a lot more than just the facts. Vast amounts of information can be googled instantly, but what is not so readily available is the wisdom to know what to *do* with the knowledge we are gaining. Where yesterday's worker made *things*, today's worker makes *decisions*, sometimes hundreds of them in a day. The higher your level of management and leadership, the more critical the decisions you're making.

This makes *wisdom* a treasured commodity, whether you're a high-powered executive making decisions that affect hundreds or thousands of employees or a busy homemaker responsible for keeping a family of five running smoothly. The best way that I've found to acquire this wisdom is by actively putting mentoring with 40:40 Principle to work in my life.

Wisdom: The ability to properly apply knowledge.

How It Works

Crystal, a thirty-year-old manager at a major corporation, typifies what most people think of when you say "rising young star." Lisa is a fifty-year-old veteran who has been with the company for most of her professional career. She has risen through the ranks to a senior executive position.

In the spirit of practical application, Crystal makes a very simple yet intentional request of Lisa by inviting her to breakfast, lunch, or a cup of coffee.

> Lisa, I have tremendous respect for your leadership skills and the way you've developed this department to be number one

---

[8]   http://mentalhealth.about.com/cs/computerstuff/a/datasmog.htm.

in the company. I would love to hear your story of how you got to this point in your career so I could learn from your experience. Could we schedule a time to do that next month?

This scenario is fairly intuitive: a young person asking for advice and mentoring from someone older. But how might the flip side look: someone older seeking help from a younger colleague?

William, forty-five years old, serves as vice president in charge of global communications at a medium-sized consumer goods company. His role this year is to upgrade and update how the company goes to market and communicates its brand and mission to a changing world and marketplace. Jason, meanwhile, is a twenty-six-year-old recently recruited programmer in the IT department of the company.

Unfortunately, William is somewhat lost when it comes to current technology. He is out of step with the latest terminology and trendy gadgets popular among the twenty-something crowd that comprises one of the company's key target markets. In the break room one Friday morning, he overhears two young employees discussing how Twitter, Facebook, Slack, and other social tools are affecting business trends. After they conclude their discussion, William fills his coffee cup and introduces himself.

I'm working on a big communications project, and I think you could help me out. I'm fairly new to the whole Twitter and Facebook thing and would love to better understand how tools like these might impact our branding and communication. Could I buy you guys lunch next week and pick your brains a little?

Such an admission and request for help from someone younger isn't nearly as intuitive and would be very difficult for many people. This type of request of an older person seeking information and insight from a younger person is counterintuitive. But it's one of the keys to maximizing the benefits of the 40:40 Principle.

CONNECTING TIP #3
Focus on being interested rather than interesting. Being interested in others will ultimately make you more interesting!

What Does Success Mean to You?

What does success look like to you? *Webster's Dictionary* defines success as "the achievement of something planned or attempted." I like to say that success is living out the vision you have for your ideal life.

Many people would agree that success is a result of having clear vision, working diligently, and creating a specific outcome. I want to suggest, however, that we often overlook the *human* element—in other words, the role that *others* play in our success. I believe this human element is the largest and most important success component, even more important than hard work. J. Paul Getty once said, "I would rather have one percent of 100 people than 100 percent of one person." I believe that *people* feed all of the other success components. So, if you are heavily focused on *your* abilities and *your* knowledge and *your* strength to succeed, you are limiting yourself. If, however, you enlist the help of other talented people, you will greatly enhance your chances of success. Many have assumed that the great Italian sculptor and painter Michelangelo worked solo, but he did not. In fact, he was assisted by thirteen other highly talented artists while creating the masterpiece on the ceiling of the Sistine Chapel in the Vatican.

Additionally, we often hear that it's not *what* you know but *who* you know that leads to success. We also are told two heads are better than one and that we are known by the company we keep. In other words, our success may depend more on who we know than anything else. Let's look at a few examples in detail to see this in real life.

NBA's two-time MVP Stephan Curry was born into basketball royalty, as the son of basketball great Dell Curry. Steph was always watching and learning "the way you handle yourself, Dad, in the NBA lifestyle… and the schedule that we have and just the stresses of the NBA life, I got to see it firsthand, up until I was about thirteen or fourteen years old. I remember those things." Steph is able to customize and model those things now, but he had to be hungry for it, as Dell told his son over the years. Steph's part was taking the initiative to ask his father questions. For example, in a vintage Burger King commercial, you see young Steph asking Dell, "What's it take to be a great basketball player like you?" Dad says, "You have to really want it, you have to be hungry for it!" Well if proof is in the pudding, Steph has become one of the best players on the planet, and in 2016 he joined President Obama at the White House to promote mentoring.

American singer-songwriter and actress Taylor Swift credits Scott Borchetta as one of her most influential mentors. Mr. Borchetta signed Taylor to Big Machine Records (before they even had the name Big Machine) when she was fourteen years old—a big risk for everyone involved. Scott noted, "She was a fascinating person, Taylor had such an amazing desire for people to like her and get to know her, and she has found a way to engage anybody whom she wants to, whether it's the immediate fan or the biggest stars in the world." He has helped guide Taylor through decisions like the open-source (free) music issue. In a *Billboard Magazine* interview, Borchetta recalls Taylor not agreeing with giving away so much free music. He outlined the reasons why: like getting a free sample of food, it makes you want more and then you will pay for it. She quickly saw the wisdom in it and agreed with the strategy.

Facebook CEO Mark Zuckerberg acknowledges former Apple Inc. CEO, the late Steve Jobs, as a key mentor. The two developed a relationship in the early days of Facebook and often met to discuss best business and management practices for the company. When Jobs passed away in the fall of 2011, Zuckerberg posted on his Facebook page, "Steve, thank you for being a mentor and a friend. Thanks for showing me that what you build can change the world. I will miss you."

Former Founder and CEO of Microsoft Bill Gates the richest man in the word, has tapped into many mentors throughout his lifetime. During childhood, his school counselor helped him put education in perspective. During his college years at Harvard, Bill wrestled with full-time attendance versus running a small software company he helped start in Albuquerque, New Mexico. He often called on his father, Bill Gates Sr., for advice on these types of issues. As the tension grew around these two competing opportunities, his father would simply listen and allow Bill to think out loud. Investing legend Warren Buffet became one of Bill's greatest mentors, helping him define vision and success. And in recent years, David Rockefeller has advised Bill on matters surrounding philanthropy and charitable foundations.

Talk show host Oprah Winfrey benefited from dozens of mentors throughout her life. Maybe her favorite was American poet, memoirist, and civil rights activist Maya Angelou. "She was there for me always, guiding me through some of the most important years of my life," Winfrey said. "Mentors are important, and I don't think anybody makes it in the world without some form of mentorship," Another was her famous fourth-grade teacher, Mrs. Mary Duncan, who encouraged her to not be afraid of being smart, and to not only read but to read the right books.[9] Another was Dr. Phil McGraw, a litigation consultant who was invited to *The Oprah Winfrey Show* to advise her in the 1998 lawsuit brought against her by the National Cattlemen's Beef Association. They claimed Oprah made derogatory comments on her show about the safety of US beef.[10] This relationship went on to become a huge win-win for both. Oprah discovered a system for teaming up with outside experts, and Dr. Phil launched his own successful self-help talk show and became a household name. More recently, Dr. Mehmet Oz, "Dr Oz," has skyrocketed in popularity as a result of offering Oprah and the world tips on diet, exercise, and all-around healthy living.

---

[9]   Harvard University, http://www.hsph.harvard.edu/chc/wmy2008/Celebrities/oprah_winfrey.html.

[10]   Released by CBS, http://www.thefutoncritic.com/news, February 12, 2008.

Each person's definition of success will be different, so it's important for you to define what you want in your life. What is success for *you*? This is important, because it will drive everything that you think and dream about, everything that you fear and doubt, and the things you will gain strategic advice about. Otherwise, you will wrestle your whole life with simply striving and surviving.

I challenge you to write down your vision for your life. Go ahead—grab a pen and paper and do it right now. It should take no longer than five minutes; you either have a vision or you don't. We often make the "vision thing" out to be a monumental exercise, when in reality, it's usually right there inside of us just waiting to be released: a passion or burden for a cause, a desire to solve a pressing problem. Let it come more from your gut than from your mind. If this exercise paralyzes you, keep reading and come back to it later— but don't forget to come back! Turn to Appendix I, "Defining your Vision of Success," in the back of this book for more guidance.

Top Ten Reasons for Those under Forty to Connect with Someone over Forty

1. Receive *career* advice.

2. Tap into *relationship* counseling (marriage, parenting, etc.).

3. Learn about *past trends* and how they may help you achieve more success today.

4. Find out how to *dress professionally* and formally when the occasion calls for it.

5. Tap into the wisdom that only comes from years of *experience* and a long-term perspective.

6. Boost your *confidence*.

7. Gain a better understanding of and empathy with your *older boss* and *coworkers*.

8. Gain a better understanding of and empathy with *your parents.*

9. Receive keen insights into achieving proper *work-life balance.*

10. Obtain a unique and deeper *spiritual perspective.*

Chapter 4

The Reward

Vision is the art of seeing what is invisible
to others. —Jonathan Swift

At this point, I hope you'll allow me to take a brief detour in order to explain the origins of the 40:40 Principle for me. I think doing so will help you see why it has transformed my life and how it can impact your life as well.

Not to get all Dr. Phil on you, but although I had a fairly normal childhood, it was overshadowed by my parents' marital dysfunction and subsequent divorce when I was eight years old. I'm sure that explains in part why I'm so open to having others speak wisdom into my life: I didn't get much of that when I was a kid. My dad was a great guy, but he poured so much of himself into his newly started business, projects around the house, and other demands a single dad faces that I missed out on many of the things other kids got from their dads. I would have loved to go on a father-son camping trip, fishing, or hunting adventure together.

Meanwhile, I had an absentee mom. She never sat down and helped me with homework, took any interest in my schoolwork or grades, or bandaged a wound (of which there were many!). My mother never prepared a home-cooked meal or baked cookies or cakes. Of my hundreds of little league games and school sports activities, I can only recall one time when she came to see me play.

Don't feel *too* sorry for me, though. I had a great extended family of uncles, aunts, and cousins. These folks made up for whatever I missed as a result of my parents splitting up. Most noteworthy was my grandmother, who stepped in physically and spiritually by tutoring, disciplining, and creating lasting memories for me. I loved it when the whole family got together, and one of my favorite times with them came at our annual family Christmas dinner at my Uncle Buck's house. Having all twenty-two of us under one roof made it seem like I was part of a real family—normal, healthy, and loving. I didn't realize it at the time, but one Christmas I got a tremendously valuable gift that would have a powerful impact on me.

The Question That Started It All

> ### CONNECTING TIP #4
> *Ask great questions: If you want a better answer, ask a better question!*

I was fifteen years old at the time, and as usual, our entire extended family had gathered at my aunt and uncle's house. As the ham baked in the oven and the house filled with irresistible aromas that intensified our hunger, the cousins would head off to the den or another part of the house to play table games or pick on each other in a good-natured way. Or, if it was one of those mild winter days in northeastern Ohio, with a fresh coating of powder, we might head outside to make a snowman—or better yet, start a snowball fight. My uncles would usually find their way to the bar and have a few holiday drinks, and my aunts joined Grandmother, the matriarch of the family, in the kitchen to get dinner ready. Soon the call would go out to everyone: "Dinner's ready!" We would politely file into the dining room and find our places around the giant mahogany table. I say politely because the only downside of these meals was that Grandmother was quite formal and expected certain decorum around the dinner table. Over the years, I had learned to decipher

her various looks that said, "Sit up straight," or, "Chew with your mouth closed," or, "Your napkin belongs in your lap."

Even with all the formality, these dinners were always a festive occasion with plenty of conversation to accompany the mountains of food. In addition to the traditional, big, golden turkey on a platter in the center of the table, almost every side dish you could imagine surrounded the bird. On this particular Christmas Day, about halfway through the meal, my grandmother posed a question to the entire table: "What is the secret to life?"

Not exactly the usual conversation starter on Christmas Day, at least not in *our* family. As a kid, I didn't know what to think in the momentary silence that followed, but I didn't have to wait long for the answer.

"That's easy," Uncle Buck said from the other end of the table. Frank B. Carr (Buck was a nickname given to him by his high school football coach) was a Renaissance man. He attended college and played football at Yale, graduated from Harvard Business School, and worked most of his life as a financier, successfully launching dozens of IPOs. "My dad, Claude Carr [Daddy Buck], used to tell me the secret to life is that when you're under forty, you need to listen to those who are *over* forty, and when you're over forty, you need to listen to those who are *under* forty."

Claude A. Carr was my grandfather. He died when I was two years old, so I never got to know him, but from all the stories about him, I knew he was a real man's man, a down-to-earth guy who liked to hunt, fish, and hang out with the guys. I may not have known him, but thanks to Uncle Buck, my grandfather would have a lifelong influence on me. Even as a teenager, I sensed the wisdom of his simple 40:40 formula—in fact, I was spellbound. As the conversation continued, I couldn't quit thinking about it. It was almost as if my grandfather was speaking wisdom into my heart from the grave.

Stop for a minute and think about it. As Bob Buford points out in his amazing book *Half Time*, when you're at the front end of your career, you're in the hunter-gatherer mode. You're in the heat of the battle, doing deals, planning strategies, and chasing your goals. Your tendency is to become self-reliant and be your own man. If you *do* develop relationships, it's usually with guys your own age. There's nothing wrong with any of this; it goes with the territory of being young and ambitious. But if you overdo the self-reliance, you'll miss the wisdom and broader perspective that comes from experience.

A wise man will hear and increase in learning, And a man of understanding will acquire wise counsel. —Proverbs 1:5

This is exacerbated in our youth-oriented culture. Unlike Asian cultures, where age is generally venerated, we North Americans tend to think when someone turns fifty, he or she doesn't have a lot to offer. Do you ever hear of a company offering a buyout to get its twentysomethings off the payroll? How shortsighted is it to nudge your valuable people out the door just to keep costs down? But it happens all the time. What my grandfather understood is that if you only hang out with people in your generation, you limit your opportunities to grow and become successful. The nineteenth-century Scottish writer Robert Louis Stevenson said it best: "To hold the same views at forty as we held at twenty is to have been stupefied for a score of years, and take rank, not as a prophet, but as an unteachable brat, well birched and none the wiser."

Why Wisdom Is a Two-Way Street

What I have found to be so unique about my grandfather's advice is that he recognized that the flow of wisdom is a two-way street. Most of us get the idea of younger people learning from those who are older. But for an older man or woman to seek wisdom from a thirty-year-old? No way! Yet think about it. If you're fifty-eight and running a small business that's losing market share, and you've been reading about e-marketing via social networking using Web 2.0 technology, do you think your best advice on this unfamiliar territory will come from the cronies you hang out with at the bar?

Again, my grandfather realized that different levels and types of wisdom come with different stages of life. Those who get ahead and stay ahead are willing to go across generational lines for wisdom, counsel, and support.

As I've adapted my grandfather's advice into a principle for personal growth and success, I've come to appreciate the fact that investing in others is as good for me as it is for them. Now that I've crossed the forty-year-old threshold, I find myself more on the giving end than the receiving end of the 40:40 Principle. It works like this.

> A young twenty-something who just got his first promotion calls and asks if he can have lunch with me. He just wants to pick my brain and run a few ideas by me. I agree, we meet at a nice restaurant, and he peppers me with questions and shares some of his dreams. I do my best to point him in the right direction by asking a lot of questions. He thanks me as we leave the restaurant and go our separate ways, and as I drive back to my office, I'm thinking, *Wow, that was inspiring! What a great kid.* I get that same feeling I used to get when I closed a big sale: high energy, An invigorating boost of well-being, food for the soul. Regardless of how busy my week is or what's on my plate when I get back to the office, the time I spent with that young man was just what *I* needed to stay invigorated.

Something else happens when I spend time engaged in spirited conversation with someone on the way up: I sharpen my own skills and reinforce all those things that have gotten me where I am today. You may have heard it said that the best way to learn something is to teach it. That's exactly what happens every time I share from my experience with others. I come away with an even greater grasp of the principles and practices that have made me successful.

A friend of mine was approaching the twenty-fifth year of his career in publishing. He'd risen up through the ranks into middle management and was made the head of his division. Although he found it gratifying to be in a position of leadership, he missed some of the hands-on work he did as a young marketing director. One day he heard a timid knock on his door and saw that a relatively new hire had sneaked past his executive assistant. Remembering his own early days at the company, he smiled and motioned for the young man to come in. The guy had been on the job for only two months and was a little nervous, but he asked my friend if he could stop by from time to time and ask a few questions about the business. They agreed to meet once a month for coffee before work, and what surprised my friend was how, once they began meeting, he found himself looking forward to each of those off-site times with this young marketing guy.

"Amid all the stress of managing budgets and making key decisions, I absolutely loved passing along what I learned over the years to this young professional," he told me. "It actually caused me to think more creatively about what I was doing now, and I approached my work with greater passion."

Believe it or not, a lot of people—especially in the corporate setting—begin to operate on autopilot when they move into the second half of their lives. There are lots of ways to keep that from happening, but thanks to my grandfather, I've discovered that if you want to stay engaged, you should seek out opportunities to share your wisdom with young people who are on the front end of their careers.

It's No Accident

You probably think you already practice the 40:40 Principle, and you may be right. Obviously, most of us can point to times when we've gone to someone older for advice, or someone younger has come to us and asked us a few questions about work, marriage, or life in general. This occasionally happens when a junior employee accompanies her supervisor on a business trip. The downtime spent in the airport, sharing a meal together, or sitting next to each other for a four-hour flight provides a lot of great face time for giving and receiving wisdom, encouragement, and support.

The only problem with these types of encounters is that they're almost accidental. There's no continuity to it, and in some cases, it can even be annoying. Imagine planning on using flight time to tweak your presentation, and this junior exec is pumping you with questions.

For the 40:40 Principle to work, it has to be *intentional.* Leave it up to chance, and there's a good chance it will never happen. Half a century ago, intentional, consistent, and challenging life-on-life relationships were built into the fabric of American culture. They took place in the home, at work, and in the church. My own experience helps illustrate the cultural shift that has made the 40:40 Principle critical to personal growth. Many families today feel the pull of busy schedules, with both parents working and isolating distractions like television, video games, and the Internet. As a young man, I craved some one-on-one quality time with my dad, but it was rare. Even our churches tended to separate people by generations and age groups so that unless we went out of our way, we were not going to interact with anyone much older or younger.

Is It Worth the Effort?

Waiting for chance encounters with wisdom givers won't get you very far down the road toward your goals and dreams. It's going to take some effort on your part, but it will pay off in huge dividends. For starters, it's not all that hard. Meeting with your own personal mentor may require nothing more from you than an invitation and a cup of coffee at Starbucks. Also, it doesn't have to be a long, drawn-out meeting. Trust me: I know you don't need another meeting, so think of this as an occasional time-out or break in your routine to help you grow. It's the one business lunch that you'll actually eagerly anticipate.

> **CONNECTING TIP #5**
> *Invest your life in others; in return others will invest in you.*

I know a man who discovered the power of these strategic relationships. He met with three younger guys individually every two weeks at a coffee shop on the way to his office. None of the young men worked for his company; he met them all through the local tennis association, where they asked for some time with him.

"I think I do it more for myself than for them," he said with a laugh. "Initially, the plan was for them to get some practical advice and counsel about the business world, and of course I shared what I knew. These guys are like sponges—they literally soak up everything I say, and it's so rewarding to know that I have a hand in shaping their careers. But, I find *I'm* learning so much from them about their generation, and that helps me lead my own company, because we have a number of employees their age. When I can't figure out which blog software is best or how to navigate the latest social media maze, I've got my own personal tech advisors!"

That's the beauty of the 40:40 Principle: it's truly a win-win for all involved. If you're under forty, you really do need a leg up on the competition. As I learned early in my career, there were a lot of people out there smarter than I was, but instead of being intimidated by them, I recognized how valuable they could be to me. The natural tendency is to be a poser and try to impress them, or to be overwhelmed and begin to think of yourself as inferior. If you're on the front end of your career, take advantage of this principle to help you get to the next level.

On the other hand, if you're over forty and maybe beginning to coast a little, give the 40:40 Principle a try. Make yourself available to a young person who's just starting out, and see what happens. I guarantee that the satisfaction you get from investing in that person, coupled with the knowledge you will pick up from them and the world they live in, will give you an invigorating jolt of emotional energy that will help you keep your competitive edge.

Before we move on, let's review the highlights of the 40:40 Principle.

- The 40:40 Principle is about creating powerful conversations with people on both sides of forty, with the goal of building intentional mentor relationships.

- If you are *under* forty years old, seek out people who are over forty, and listen to them.

- If you are *over* forty years old, seek out people who are under forty, and listen to them.

- Remember that wisdom, encouragement, and support flow both ways. Be willing to give as well as receive.

One of the clearest thoughts describing this profound concept comes from the great playwright Tennessee Williams: "Life is partly what we make of it, and partly what it is made by the friends we choose."

Think about It

- How would you answer this question: What is the secret to life?

- My uncle said the secret to life is seeking wisdom: when you're under forty, listen to those over forty, and when you're over forty, listen to those under forty. What is your initial reaction to the 40:40 Principle?

- I gave the example of a mutually beneficial relationship between an older businessman and three young professionals. How could a strategic relationship like this, with someone much older or much younger, benefit you?

Chapter 5

Mentor-less

Too much of what is called "education" is little more than
an expensive isolation from reality. —Thomas Sowell

I got my big start in the business world when I was twelve years
old. I saw this kid I knew mowing someone else's lawn and asked
him, "Why are you mowing *their* lawn?" When he told me he was
being *paid* to mow their lawn, I was incredulous at first. "You mean
they're actually paying you to mow their lawn?" When he nodded,
a light bulb went off in my head. Up to that point in my young
life, mowing the lawn was something you did because your parents
told you to. They didn't pay you—you just did it. And when you
got done, you joined your buddies at the ball field. You didn't mow
someone else's lawn.

Before the end of the day, I was in business, and I didn't stop
at mowing lawns. My "company" also raked leaves in the fall and
shoveled snow in the winter. I quickly discovered that these jobs gave
me money to buy the things I wanted. I'd hear other kids complain
because they didn't have a new bicycle or baseball glove. I used to
complain too, but almost overnight I became a "make it happen"
kind of kid. When I wanted something and didn't have enough
money for it, I'd just find more work and the money followed.

By the time I got into college at Kent State University, I was
practically a veteran when it came to running a business. No one

who knew me was surprised when I started a full-fledged house-painting business to not only help pay my college bills but let me live just a little bit better than the average student. While all they could afford were ramen noodles, I was able to upgrade to ramen noodles with freeze-dried vegetables! I was learning an important lesson that would follow me throughout my career: if you really want or need something, you can have it if you're willing to work for it.

When it came time to walk across the platform and get my cherished college diploma, I knew exactly what I wanted to do with my life: get rich. Okay, maybe that was what everybody wanted to do, but at least *I* had a plan in place that would have me living the good life sooner rather than later. I was going to buy and sell real estate by finding something cheap and ugly, fixing it up, and then selling it for a profit. My experience running the house-painting business helped point me toward real estate. I loved the transformation that took place when my paint crew finished a house. What was drab and unappealing became beautiful and attractive. Imagine the money I could make if I bought an old building, rehabbed it, and then put it on the market. And then maybe I'd buy an entire city block and turn it into a mall. As far as I was concerned, there was a fortune to be made in real estate, and two books further convinced me that this was where I belonged: *The Art of the Deal* by Donald Trump and *Nothing Down* by Robert Allen. Both books whetted my appetite to begin doing deals. I could hardly wait to buy my first piece of property.

Hitting a Detour

For reasons I still don't fully understand, I decided to move back home and take a job in my father's business. I know what you're thinking: rich kid, born with a silver spoon in his mouth, can't resist taking the easy way to make his fortune. I wish. My dad was a hard-working guy who owned his own business, but it wasn't exactly a gold mine. It was a machine tool business in a transitional area of Cleveland, Ohio—more of a sales organization where we supplied new and used heavy machinery (lathes, presses, grinders, and boring mills) to hundreds of factories and tool and die shops in the region.

During the last semester of my senior year at Kent State, I interviewed with dozens of recruiters who came to our campus, and I was even offered a few really sweet jobs at companies like Proctor and Gamble, Pillsbury, and Carolina Freight. But here I was in a drab, dreary, dark, little office with a greasy desk and a battered file cabinet. I hate to say it, but the place even smelled bad: diesel fuel mixed with bearing grease. What was I thinking?

In retrospect, it was a great detour. I stayed just long enough to understand what I needed in order to be successful, and I owe a lot to my dad's sales manager. But probably not in the way you'd expect.

Dan Simmons (not his real name) had been with the company for a long time, and apparently he felt it was his responsibility to take me under his wing and show me the ropes of industrial sales. Even though I felt my business experiences and college classes taught me a lot about selling, I was eager to learn from a pro. When Dan invited me to join him for breakfast with a client to show me how to make a sales pitch, I readily accepted.

We left the office around 8:30, hopped into his fifteen-year-old clunker, and headed to Denny's to meet our client. I know what you're thinking: Denny's? In a clunker? It should have set off warning bells in my brain, but I was focused on seeing this guy in action. I wanted to learn how a veteran sales guy made a pitch to a potentially lucrative customer.

CONNECTING TIP #6
Don't make something that is clear, unclear. If it looks like a duck, acts like a duck and sounds like a duck, then it's a duck!

We got to the restaurant, ordered our Grand Slams, and engaged in small talk. I was wondering how he was going to move the conversation from baseball to turret grinders. If there was a transition, I missed it. Somewhere between my second cup of coffee and the last piece of bacon, Dan delivered the fastball right out of the blue.

"Hey, Joe, do you think you can buy something from me today?"

I felt like I was sitting at the table with Danny DeVito and Richard Dreyfuss in *Tin Men,* that hilarious movie about two guys who do all the wrong things while trying to sell aluminum siding to homeowners. Of course, Dan had asked no qualifying questions or attempted to discern his needs, and so Joe's answer didn't surprise me one bit. "No thanks, Dan, I have everything I need right now."

Undaunted, Dan kicked it into high gear. "Aw, come on, Joe. Please? Can't you buy *something* from us? Anything?"

By now I was embarrassed but also a little confused. After all, this was the real world. Dan had been doing this for more than thirty years. Maybe he knew something I hadn't learned in college. Maybe this was a selling strategy that delivered results. If so, it wasn't working. Joe wouldn't budge.

That was when Dan unleashed his final assault, and I realized I was in the wrong job and would have to leave my father's business. As Joe made it clear he was ready to leave, Dan launched into what I now call the "Tijuana street beggar sales strategy." He literally begged Joe to buy something, anything! I couldn't believe what I was seeing: a grown man literally begging a quality client to do a deal. I learned in college that you need to qualify your potential clients, open the dialogue, give relevant information, assess the level of interest, and then (if there is a strategic fit) attempt to close the deal.

Dan did none of that, and we left the restaurant with nothing to show for our meeting besides indigestion and the bill. So I headed west, literally.

Go West, Young Man

Despite my dad's disappointment that I had chosen to leave the family business, I packed all my belongings into my 1977 Chevrolet Monte Carlo and drove to San Diego, stopping at rest areas along the way to get some sleep at night in my car. I had a friend in San Diego who let me crash on the living room floor of his apartment that he shared with four other guys until I found a job. But I set my sights pretty high: I would only work for a Fortune 500–caliber company.

A friend of a friend set up an interview for me with Coldwell Banker, a major national real estate company that fit my criteria, and I was immediately offered a job with this caveat: "The sky's the limit out here, and you will be making a lot of money, but it's going to take you six months before you start earning anything." This was in La Jolla, and I couldn't have known that over the next few years, the market there would boom.

I had about four hundred dollars to my name, and the prospect of being poor for the next six months wasn't very appealing, so I turned them down. In retrospect, it looks like a poor financial decision, but I now believe it was actually wise—and perhaps evidence that somebody was looking out for me. I've seen what happens to young people who start making big money early in their careers, and had I taken that job, I might be really rich but also completely miserable. But ironically, even though I was unwilling to wait six months to start making money, it took me almost that long to land a quality job.

I was about to give up and head back east when I got an interview with E. & J. Gallo, the winemakers. To be honest, my expectations were pretty low, and it didn't help when I showed up at their Los Angeles headquarters, which was a tired old warehouse in a nondescript industrial strip. I figured I was overqualified for the job being offered and half expected to meet a West Coast version of Dan Simmons. Yet the minute I walked into the building, I started to think the opposite. Maybe I had finally found the company I was looking for—or maybe I had gotten in over my head! The folks at Gallo had transformed the interior of this old warehouse into a world-class suite of offices and meeting space. The place was gorgeous inside.

But what impressed me the most were the people. Everyone I met, from the receptionist to the top sales executive, exuded confidence. My sense of being overqualified further evaporated when I learned that the two men I would be working with both had MBAs, one from USC and the other from Harvard. I was thrilled when they offered me the job, not so much because of the money but because I knew it would be a place where I could learn and grow. Both the sales manager and the head of the division I worked in became mentors to me. They seemed genuinely interested in helping me grow and succeed.

Learning from a Real Pro

Shortly after I started, one of my colleagues, Pete Overland, invited me to join him for a sales presentation at a major grocery store in Encinitas. I jumped at the chance, thinking this would be a great opportunity to learn from a pro. His goal was to sell a fifty-case wine display. He started out talking with our client about his family and how his store was doing—basically anything except wine. I saw another train wreck coming and started to look for the exit when Pete cut right to the chase.

"Jim, do you need a 150-case display or a 100-case display?"

To my great surprise, Jim replied, "Let's cut it down the middle, Pete. I'll take 125. See you Monday morning."

When I asked Pete about his presentation later that day, he explained that he had three options when he approached his client: rush into the sales conversation, overpresent with too many facts and figures (that would have been my approach), or develop the relationship and ask for the sale. It's what I have come to call trust-based selling. From Pete I learned that *relationships drive results.*

But what I really learned from him and everyone at E. & J. Gallo is that *wisdom and encouragement from others* are the real drivers of personal success. Within a relatively short period of time at the company, I received two big promotions that were a direct result of Pete and our division manager, Greg Brown, investing in me with their time and advice. Once over lunch with Greg, I asked him what it would take to advance to the next level of leadership, and he never answered any of my questions. Instead, he asked *me* questions that forced me to discover the answer to my questions, rather than just blindly follow his advice—Socratic leadership at its best. It showed a level of trust and confidence in me that I had never experienced.

Eventually I realized I needed to learn more about the rest of the beverage industry, so I left Gallo to take a position with Veryfine Products, the makers of Veryfine Juice and flavored water. During my second year, sales declined across the company due to competition from bottled water manufacturers and other fruit juice rivals. In an unusual move, the president of the company challenged the sales managers to come up with new product ideas.

I was driving on the interstate in Boston with a colleague, Jim McKinnon, on our way to a sales meeting. We got to talking about our boss's challenge and came up with a new product idea: what if we took bottled water to another level? Add some fruit flavoring and a little artificial sweetener; Veryfine had exclusive rights to using the Splenda brand sweetener for two years. You'd still have the no-calorie benefit of bottled water, but it was not as boring. The company loved the idea, and Fruit2O was born! The success of that product led to a job running a $25 million division of yet another major beverage company. By the time I was thirty-seven years old, I had accomplished two of the primary career goals I had set for myself: launch a national brand and run a $25 million business. Although I didn't realize it at the time, I was beginning to see the 40:40 Principle at work.

I share all of this because my experience cuts against a lot of what you may have learned about success: that it's not all about *you*. You don't have to step on other people's hands as you climb the ladder of success. In fact, you're far less likely to be successful and achieve your goals if you try to do it on your own.

Think about It

- In this chapter, I shared some of my story and described key people who led me on the right career track. Think about some of your crucial decisions in life. Who helped you along the way and influenced your choices?

- This is a well-known phrase: "If it's to be, it's up to me." Do you feel alone or supported in the most important areas of your life? Consider work, spiritual health, finances, physical fitness, marriage, and parenting.

- You don't have to step on people as you climb the ladder of success. In fact, you're far less likely to achieve your goals if you try to do it on your own.

Chapter 6

Better Than Self-Help

Isolation is a dream killer. —Barbara Sher

We are all familiar with the concept of self-help. The self-help movement grew out of people's desires to find an easy way to improve different areas of their lives, whether it was their health, relationships, spirituality, or careers. Through self-help, a lot of people have become more empowered. Self-help concepts are usually introduced as epiphanies that are meant to better our lives.

Millions of self-help tools are sold each year, and I have purchased many of them myself. But recently, it hit me that they may not be delivering the results I hoped for. For example, not long ago I rounded up a large stack of self-help books and workbooks I had read, and it measured nearly two feet tall! I carried them with me into an early morning meeting with my ten-member affinity group of fellow business owners and slammed them down on the boardroom table. "So," I asked them, "how many of you are fed up with your stack of books at home or at work that promised incredible change but just don't deliver?"

Self-help books and other tools often give us that great up-front burst of energy so we can say, "At last, I have the formula!" Then a day or two later, when the afterglow wanes and the bloom is off the rose, we find ourselves reverting to our old behaviors. Stumped at what to do next, we look for the next self-help book, concept, or seminar.

My point is not to question whether self-help tools work. For some people they do, and for others they don't. But is it enough just to buy the book, CD, or DVD, or to go to the conference or seminar? Could these self-help tools make more of an impact if, along with them, we were to add mentors to our lives?

Like all things in life, self-help, self-service, or self-anything has its limitations. One of the biggest is the focus it puts on the self (big surprise), as opposed to the self *and* others. We often believe the notion that self is sufficient, and we can be complete apart from others. However, I suggest that others are the reason why we are alive on this earth. In today's isolated, chaotic, fragmented, information-overloaded society, many feel the need to get reconnected and be face-to-face with other people. For you, this may be someone with practical life experience who has lived through your circumstances (and who is probably over forty), or someone with next-generation fresh eyes to see what you can't (and who is probably under forty).

Truth be told, I believe that the whole idea of self-help is inherently flawed because it is based on formulas that *limit* one's wisdom rather than expand it. The self-help approach often delivers some initial results, but it usually requires a seemingly never-ending succession of new approaches and formulas if you want to enjoy long-term success. I believe that true success in any area of your life will only come through the establishment of intentional, strategic relationships.

So, what does all this mean to you? How can you start moving from self-help to *beyond* self-help? How can you put the communication and relationship revolution that's brewing around us to work to benefit you?

Two Styles of Learning

The self-help style of learning is generally characterized by receiving information passively such as reading books and attending seminars. What I call the "beyond self-help" concept, however, is characterized more by a different style of learning that's more *experiential* and fueled by a relational-coach approach. I suggest that our real need is for this experiential style of learning, specifically people connecting face-to-face and life-on-life. We do not need more and more information void of human interaction. If we did, Amazon would have run Barnes and Noble out of business by now, and Starbucks could survive with just their drive-through window.

So, how did we get to this place where passive information is king and the experiential (or people) part of learning has taken a backseat? Let's take a brief look back at how humankind has learned throughout history. Prior to AD 100, most of the world operated on the Hebrew model of learning, which is a relational, experiential approach. However, this all changed during the first century through Greek and Roman influence. At this time, much of the civilized world migrated to the Greek model of learning, which is more of a passive, academic, and classroom-based approach. Note the differences between these two models.

STYLES OF LEARNING

Western (Greek)	vs.	Eastern (Hebraic)
INFORMATION / SELF-HELP		**PEOPLE / BEYOND SELF-HELP**
"The Classroom Model"		"The Coach Model"
Academic		Relational
Passive		Experiential
Theoretical		Practical, on-the-job training
What school did you attend?		Who was your mentor?

Don't get me wrong: there is nothing inherently wrong with the Greek/classroom style of learning. It has many advantages, as does the Hebrew style, and to choose one over the other is unnecessary. We need both, but I would argue that the Hebrew/coach model is needed even more in today's information-saturated world. We need it primarily to help us navigate through the mountains of information (and misinformation) we must process every day. It seems in today's culture, we want to spend less time with more people (think e-mail, texting, tweeting, and so on), but history tells us that the best way to grow personally and professionally is to spend *more* time with *fewer* people. Relationship-wise, most of us have indeed become a mile wide and an inch deep.

But the good news is that you don't have to settle for a relationally shallow life. In order to truly advance your life toward success while enjoying life along the way, engage or expand the Hebrew/coach approach to learning.

Which Style Do You Prefer?

Think about yourself. Do you tend to prefer a coach or a classroom, an individual or information? As I stated earlier: "More people prefer a guide by their side than a sage on the stage." However, most of us have been trained in assembly-line fashion as cookie-cutter workers who have learned much theory but little application. This system has limitations for producing healthy, balanced, and productive people.

Most of the Greek/classroom models of instruction are conducted in large-group formats so that information can be conveyed to as many people as possible at one time. Large events like this (see event/ process chart below) are great forums for getting everybody pumped up and motivated—just think about your favorite self-help seminar, whether it's a Tony Robbins mega-event, an annual conference you attend for work, or a seminar where you learn more about your favorite hobby or pastime. However, we need some kind of ongoing process to inspire the kind of personal development that breeds trust and authenticity (within the mix of relationships). That is what people are hungry for today.

As you review the particulars of these two styles of learning, remember the application: to connect with one person older than you and one person younger in order to take the 40:40 Principle for a test drive.

Events (one-time)	*vs.*	Process (ongoing)
EVENTS		**PROCESS**
Encourages decisions		Encourages development
Motivates people		Matures people
Usually a large group		Usually a small group or 1-1
Challenges people		Changes people
Becomes a catalyst		Becomes a culture
Easy		Difficult

The 40:40 Challenge

Think of the 40:40 Principle as a challenge to add not more random people into your life, but mentors who can help direct or redirect you, inspire you, and challenge you. In *The 7 Habits of Highly Effective People*, Steven Covey put it this way.

> Create opportunities to interact one-on-one with your boss, your children, your spouse, your friends, and your employees. When you listen, you learn, which opens the door to creative solutions and mutual trust.[11]

This can take the form of one-on-one relationships with individual mentors or team relationships with groups of three to fifteen advisors whom you meet with either in person or over the telephone. In addition, you could augment this time by viewing videos or listening to CDs or podcasts from teachers, trainers, motivational speakers, and so on. It's important to note that these virtual and electronic opportunities shouldn't replace human relationships; rather, they should *enhance* them and serve as another type of mentor. In the diagram below, you can see three primary ways to connect with life-changing mentors beyond the written

---

[11] Stephen R. Covey, *The 7 Habits of Highly Effective People*, part III, habit #5.

word; face-to-face (in person), ear-to-ear (telephone), or cloud based (webinar, video, or audio).

One of the most relevant voices over the past century in the field of human relationships was Dale Carnegie. In 1937, he wrote *How to Win Friends and Influence People*, which became an overnight sensation and has since sold more than fifteen million copies. My biggest takeaway from the book is simple: stop talking and start listening!

Six Steps to More Powerful Conversations

1. Become genuiniely interested in other people
2. Use the person's name when talking with them
3. Listen well, encouraging others to talk about themselves
4. Ask about their interests, rather than talking about yours
5. Make others feel important - and do so sincerely
6. Smile, often

For some of you, moving in this direction will be a huge challenge. For others, it will be a great reminder to reengage in something you may have allowed busyness to crowd out. If meeting with other people in this way is a stretch for you, I want to encourage you to reach beyond your comfort level and just do it.

If you invite a mentor to sit down with you at a coffee shop, you don't need a formal process for talking. Don't let the unpredictability of an informal meeting dissuade you from aggressively seeking out such a person. I have found that not much more than "Tell me about …" gets the conversation going, and usually both parties are checking their watches an hour later, surprised that the time has passed so quickly. Why is this? Because conversation naturally happens. For a list of questions to help stimulate great conversations, turn to Appendix IV at the end of this book.

> ## CONNECTING TIP #7
> *Be willing to listen. The great talk show host Larry King has said, "I've never learned anything with my mouth open"*

Remember that having a conversation is not complicated. Most of us, if we're really honest, would say we were better at conversation in grade school than we are today. So what changed? Why are many of us so intentional about producing results, but we're so unintentional about developing people or building strategic relationships?

How Does It Look in Real Life?

How might something like this materialize for you? Well, if you are a junior executive, you could invite a CEO to spend thirty minutes telling you the story of how he or she navigated from the mailroom to the boardroom. Conversely, if you are an experienced executive, consider inviting a college recruit to lunch to ask his or her opinion on a new product rollout or expansion. The feedback may shed light on new strategies you haven't considered that could save thousands of dollars or increase your market share.

Here's another potential scenario. A young mother who's feeling a bit overwhelmed could invite a more seasoned mom (whether it's a neighborhood friend or favorite aunt) out to breakfast. The conversation could start out talking about food or cooking or laundry, but eventually it'll move into more serious areas like balancing the demands of motherhood, marriage, and work.

Here's one more example with a different twist. My wife and I love to invest our time and energy in mentoring newly married couples. This is partly because we never received this kind of mentoring early in our marriage and have since come to realize how valuable it can be. We also see the tremendous growth potential young couples have during the honeymoon stage of their marriage. Most Monday nights, Nikki and I have the privilege of putting our twenty-one years of marriage to use by helping (or "strategically advising") five just-married couples navigate the myriad issues that can come up during the first year of marriage. The cool part is that we get just as much, if not more, out of being part of this group as they do.

Don't let age, stage of life, or anything else that might be superficial limit your desire to connect with and learn from others. The most important qualification is simple: is this individual *wise*? The answer will usually come to you instantly based on the person's lifestyle, background, and history. Trust your instincts and gravitate toward wise people—and away from those who are unwise.

How do you distinguish between wise and unwise people? Here's one way: consider whether this person has a consistent track record or history of making wise decisions, as evidenced by his or her lifestyle. Don't let someone's fancy title or image outweigh the facts. You deserve substance, not pomp and circumstance, when choosing the mentors who will help guide your life.

Do you already have mentors in your life? If so, great. But are you being *intentional* with them? And are they *really* wise? If you have to think about it, they probably aren't. Turn the volume down with unwise people, or shut off the radio completely and strive to surround yourself only with people who pass the wisdom test. Meanwhile, if you don't currently have any mentors in your life, start by identifying two or three wise individuals, and talk to them about meeting once either one-on-one or as part of a team to test-drive the possibilities. We'll discuss the concept of mentor teams in more detail in chapter 8.

Got Practical Wisdom?

You have probably tried many different things to help you live the life you have always wanted and with whatever it is that success means to you. You have read the right books, gone to the right seminars and conferences, attended the right churches, seen the right gurus, and so forth. Still, within days if not weeks afterward, it was back to the same old, same old.

It's not that any of these activities are wrong; they are simply incomplete. The 40:40 Principle gives you support between the books, training, and seminars to help you build upon the excitement and enthusiasm that were ignited during one of these catalysts. The 40:40 Principle does not replace other helpful tools—it enhances them!

A few years ago, I flew across the country to interview some of the nation's top authors on the subject of leadership. I asked them one basic question: What are the best techniques and training when it comes to influencing and growing leaders? To my surprise, every single one of them gave me the same answer.

> The best way to influence and grow a leader is not with books, seminars, workshops, sermons, or DVDs, but by building, nurturing, and maintaining *life-on-life relationships.*

In other words, it's spending consistent quality time with mentors. All the tools we've mentioned are helpful, but according to these experts, the number one way to positively influence others (and be positively influenced yourself) is to experience life with other people who are focused on the same things and headed in the same direction as you are.

I recently invited twelve highly influential leaders of organizations and teams to participate in a leadership roundtable. During the meeting, I posed one key question: What is the main thing your employees and associates are asking from you? The top response was not more money or time off; it was more *personal investment* in them. People wanted to spend more time with their leaders, the individuals who could help equip, guide, and coach them up to the next level.

It's obvious to me that the need is there. I'm sensing that although many of us *want* to make these vital connections, we still let other, more "urgent" matters push this off our priority list.

Think about It

- Recall the last self-help tool you utilized by *yourself,* such as a book, CD, or seminar, that led to a positive, permanent change in your life. Would your chances of success increase with a wise person walking alongside you for motivation, support, and accountability?

- Are your relationships a mile wide and an inch deep? The best way to grow personally and professionally is to spend more time with fewer people.

- What urgent matters take priority in your life and put people on the backburner?

Chapter 7

Can You Really Learn from Someone Younger?

If we don't change, we don't grow. If we don't
grow, we are not really living. —Gail Sheehy

Most people easily grasp the idea of learning from those who are older and more experienced, but it's easy to stumble over the younger generation part of the 40:40 Principle. In fact, one of the biggest questions I hear from people when I talk to them about the 40:40 Principle is that although the idea of learning from a mentor who's older makes sense, they're not so sure they can learn very much from someone younger—especially someone who is a decade or more younger.

Hey, I hear ya! I was pretty skeptical at first, too. But here's a quick story about how I first learned the value of being open to gaining wisdom from someone (much) younger than I.

I've played a little tennis off and on throughout my life, and though I've never considered myself a super serious player, I wouldn't call myself a hacker either. A few years ago, a friend of mine named Rick challenged me to a match. I was a little rusty, but as a competitive guy, I replied, "Sure, why not?" Rick obviously wasn't rusty at all—he waxed me 6-0, 6-0, 6-0.

Now, I am highly competitive (did I mention that yet?), so I said to him, "Great playing, Rick. How about a rematch next weekend?" *Surely I can do better than that,* I thought. Nope—Rick goose-egged me again. In six sets of tennis, I hadn't won a single game off this guy!

My competitive pride was seriously wounded, so I decided I would do everything in my power to beat him. I have been able to overcome impossible odds time and time again in many different areas of my life, so I figured this shouldn't too hard. I went out, bought a top-of-the-line tennis racquet and some high-tech shoes, and started practicing during the week, running to get better conditioned—anything to get an edge on Rick.

It paid off, a little. The next week, I took one game out of six. A few more weeks went by, and in frustration I said to a different friend, "I've done everything I can, and I don't think I can improve any more. This guy still annihilates me. I admit defeat. I cannot fix myself beyond this point."

"Have you ever worked with a tennis coach?" my friend asked.

That's when it hit me: I was stuck on what I could do in and of *myself.* I had not thought beyond me, myself, and I. I scheduled a lesson at the Stone Mountain Tennis Center in Atlanta, the site of the 1996 Olympic tennis competition. But when I arrived and met my coach, I was immediately disappointed—he looked no older than a teenager! *Are you kidding me?* I thought. *What can this kid teach me?* I wanted someone with a little gray hair and years of experience and knowledge.

As it turned out, the "kid" was a tennis whiz—a high school state champ and college superstar. We worked on three things that he said would change my game if I applied them: my grip, my stroke, and my footwork. I accepted his teaching and fully engaged the techniques. True to his promise, my game worsened short-term, but within three weeks I began to see drastic changes.

A month later, I played Rick again, but this time I was brimming with confidence. The first two sets were tight, but I pulled both of them out by scores of 6-4, 6-4. With the tension mounting, we moved into the third set and my opportunity for a sweep. In full Olympic glory, I took the third set 6-1 and completed the sweep of my tennis nemesis.

I was on top of the world, and all because I listened to someone who had wisdom beyond mine in a particular area—*and* who was twelve years younger. I had always understood the part of the 40:40 Principle about learning from older people; that's intuitive for most of us. But I was finally beginning to grasp the second part of the 40:40 Principle in a real and personal way.

A Not-so-Smart Move

Here's another story in a negative light from earlier in my life that helps illustrate the power of learning from those younger than you, or what problems could have been avoided with the help of mentors. When I was fourteen, my best friend, Tom, announced that his family was moving from Ohio to Alabama. His dad, Frank, who was forty-seven years old, was laid off from the company he'd worked for most of his life. Frank decided this was his opportunity to strike out on his own, so he bought six used mainframe computers from his former employer and decided to start his own computer business in Mobile.

This was in the 1970s, before the PC had been invented and everything was done on those mammoth mainframes that were big enough to fill a small room. As we know now, the PC revolution was just a few years away. Even though I was fourteen, I remember wondering if Frank knew what he was doing. Well, I was recruited to help Tom and Frank move the computers from the high-rise office building in downtown Cleveland, where he'd bought them, to their garage out in the suburbs. *If this big technology company is getting rid of these massive computers for newer models, what could they really be worth?* I thought. They looked like landfill material to me. I remember overhearing how much money he'd paid for them, and it was a lot, but he had decided this was going to be his future. This whole thing didn't make sense even in my teenage brain. *But what do I know?* I said to myself. *I'm fourteen, and he's forty-seven.*

A year later, Tom was back in Ohio again. It turns out the computers Frank bought *were* miserably outdated and of little value to anyone. His business in Alabama never got off the ground, and Frank lost all his money in the venture. Broke, dejected, and humiliated, he moved his family back to our hometown and tried to start over again. Not even fifty years old yet, Frank should have had a good twenty-five or thirty years left in his battery pack. Instead, he ended up a depressed shell of the man he had been before he'd struck out on his ill-fated business venture.

Now think about this: what might Frank's life have looked like if, before he bought those old mainframes, he had invited a wise twenty-seven-year-old to lunch to pick his brain about new technology trends and skills? What if he had asked him what he thought was going to happen in the computer industry over the next five or ten years? Could he have picked up a few insights that might have shed some light on where the industry was headed before forking over thousands of dollars for dinosaur mainframes?

Was it pride that kept Frank from seeking outside counsel from mentors who might have helped him avoid his disastrous decision? I don't know. But I do know that although his goal was to finish strong, he ended up scoring a DNF: did not finish. Don't let this happen to you. Engage wise mentors who are both older *and* younger than you and who finish strong.

Still Skeptical?

Perhaps my learning from a young tennis pro and having a little bit of foresight about a failed business when I was fourteen isn't enough to convince you that you can learn from someone younger. Here are a few examples of well-known people who accomplished extraordinary things before they reached the age of forty.

- Steve Jobs was twenty-one years old when he cofounded Apple Computers. After pioneering the Apple I and the Apple II with Steve Wozniak, they launched the game-changing Macintosh, and personal electronics have not been the same since.

- Bill Gates was twenty-four years old when he helped IBM launch the DOS operating system, leading to the formation of Microsoft and a personal fortune of billions for Mr. Gates, who is now the richest man in the world—and one of the most generous.

- Thomas Edison was thirty-two years old when he took the idea of the incandescent lamp and invented the lightbulb. This is just one of his hundreds of patented inventions, but it's the one that changed the course of the world in the late nineteenth century.

- Oprah Winfrey was thirty-two years old when she began using her life lessons to launch her career as a TV talk show host and eventual movie actress. She is now the most wealthy and powerful woman in the entertainment industry, overseeing a media empire that spans TV, movies, publishing, the Internet, and more.

- Jesus of Nazareth was thirty years old when he started his ministry in the Roman-occupied territory we now know as Israel. In just three short years, he laid the foundation for what would become the most influential religion in the history of the world.

If you're over forty, who do you know from the younger generation who's clued in to the current culture, modern trends, and new technology—someone who could possibly provide invaluable perspective beyond your limited viewpoint? In this age of rapidly changing information and technology, it is even more critical to seek the perspective of those younger than us if we want to compete at the highest level.

Top Ten Reasons for Those over Forty to Connect with Someone Under Forty

1. Learn more about the *technology* of the day.
2. Get a primer on current *terminology*, or a "lingo update."
3. Get up to speed on the latest *trends*.

4. Get a *relevance* reality check. In other words, are you still relevant today?

5. Find out about current *fashions,* because you could be wearing clothes that are fifteen years out of date!

6. Receive a healthy dose of *optimism* and *positivity.*

7. Draw off of the person's *vitality* and *youthful energy.*

8. Gain a better understanding of and empathy with *your children.*

9. Gain a better understanding of and empathy with *your young employees.*

10. Be challenged to improve your *health* and *physical fitness.*

Think about It

*   What is your initial reaction to the thought of learning from a mentor who is a decade younger than you?

*   When you read the story about Frank's failed business, what came to your mind?

*   Who do you know from the younger generation that is clued into the current culture, modern trends, and new technology?

Chapter 8

Real Life: 40:40 Success Stories

Connecting with others is a brain to pick, an ear to
listen, and a push in the right direction. —John Crosby

Right now, you might be wondering whether there are any real
life examples of how the 40:40 Principle and mentors have helped
real people (other than your humble author) reach their goals and
achieve success. I'm glad you asked!

Bono: Early Influences Pay Off

Paul David Hewson—better known as Bono, the lead singer
for the rock supergroup U2—grew up in Dublin, Ireland, where he
attended Mount Temple Comprehensive Secondary School in the
late 1970s. He could have been lured in any number of directions
during his school days, but fortunately he connected with some
exemplary mentors very early in his life.

One of them was Jack Heaslip, a respected teacher at the school
who offered Bono support and encouragement. Heaslip and Bono
stayed so close that he performed Bono's marriage to Ali Hewson and
has even toured with the band in recent years. Another influential
person was Don Moxham, one of Bono's teachers at the secondary
school. Although Mr. Moxham's main role was as a history professor,
he also developed relationships with his students and struck up

a friendship with the boys in U2, with whom he had many long talk sessions. Moxham believed that teaching via what he called informal interconnections was just as important as teaching in the classroom.[12]

I believe that part of U2 and Bono's success and longevity lies in the strategic relationships they formed with these and other advisors during their formative years, and the fact that they have maintained ongoing relationships with many of them to this day. Most popular rock stars and celebrities are too proud and too busy to make room for people like this in their lives, but Bono's story illustrates the ultimate success that doing so can yield.

Ben Roethlisberger: A Rookie's Mentor

During the 2009 football season, the Pittsburgh Steelers won a record sixth Super Bowl, more than any other NFL team in history. What's even more remarkable is that the Steelers' young quarterback, Ben Roethlisberger, won two Super Bowls (2006 and 2009) in his first six years in the league. He is only the second quarterback in league history to win two Super Bowls before reaching the age of twenty-six (the other is Tom Brady of the New England Patriots).

But there's a good chance Ben wouldn't rise to the occasion so masterfully without the mentorship of Jerome Bettis, aka "The Bus." Jerome was ten years older than Ben, and he could have easily snubbed the new upstart and let Ben figure out everything on his own. Conversely, Ben could have joined the team as a cocky young gun, top draft pick with no perceived need for the likes of a role-playing (and even non-starting at this late stage in his career) running back. But neither acted this way. In fact, to hear Ben talk about Jerome is inspiring. "There's many times, and I know this sounds crazy, people wear those bracelets that say, 'What Would Jesus Do?' There's times when I think, *How would Jerome handle this?*"

Ben recalls how the connection began, on his first day with the team in 2004, after the Steelers drafted him as the eleventh pick of the first round of the NFL draft. He was carrying his playbook and a

---

[12]   Steve Stockman, *Walk on-U2* (Relevant Media Group, 2005), 16–19.

notebook, and Jerome walked up to him and grabbed the notebook. "He writes 'Jerome,'" Ben says. "He writes 'home number' and 'cell number.' And he goes, 'Anything you need, I have. Anything you want, I have. If you ever want to go out. Anything you ever need, just give me a call. Don't hesitate to call me.'" Ben called, and the first time they hung out together at Ben's house, they talked for hours. "We talked about everything from how to deal with people, the media, how to equal out your time between your teammates, don't show favoritism one way or another," Ben says.

After Ben's first year, Jerome said he was going to retire from football, but he came back so he could play with Ben one more year. With Ben, he believed the Steelers had a good chance to not only deliver his first championship but also that long-elusive "one for the thumb" for the franchise. "That was unbelievable for him to say something like that to me and the confidence he instilled in me with that. I know that he's always there. No matter what it is, if I need to call him, I can call him."[13]

This is the power of inviting wise people into your life: they will encourage, inspire, and support you. We would all love to have something as unique as the relationship between Ben Roethlisberger and Jerome Bettis. Most of us will not have the opportunity to play professional football, but we can be open to these opportunities when they come along (like Ben was), or we can invest in others who need what we have to offer (like Jerome did).

Bob Buford: The Mentor of a Lifetime

Bob Buford's story of connecting with mentors is especially inspiring to me. Until the sale of his company in 1999, Bob served as chairman of the board and CEO of Buford Television, Inc., a family-owned business that started with a single ABC affiliate in Tyler, Texas, and grew to a network of cable systems across the country. He cofounded the Leadership Network in 1984 and became founding chairman in 1988 of what was initially called the Peter F.

---

[13]   ESPN NFL, January 17, 2006, by Michael Smith, posted online.

Drucker Foundation for Nonprofit Management. Bob popularized the concept of halftime through the publication of several books.

What inspires me about Bob is his unrelenting pursuit of mentors. He did it the hard way by going after them himself. It wasn't easy, but it has paid off for him. His greatest find, in my opinion, was Peter F. Drucker, the author of thirty-nine books on business, government, and nonprofit management, and who is widely considered to be the father of modern management.

This mentor had such an effect on Bob that it's unusual to spend more than an hour with Bob and not hear about Peter Drucker. What specifically did Peter do for Bob? Bob says Peter helped him in eight key learning areas.

1. He defined the lay of the land: current social and economic trends.

2. He helped define current problems (opportunities) and solutions and what was needed at that time to solve them.

3. He helped to clarify Bob's strengths and capabilities.

4. He identified the myths and false paths within the industry Bob was working in.

5. He encouraged Bob to go for it.

6. He helped Bob strategize.

7. He celebrated results with Bob.

8. He pointed out Bob's wasted effort.

Bob says his life would be considerably different had it not been for Peter. Noteworthy to me is the fact that Peter did not come beating down Bob's door; rather, Bob had to pursue Peter and prove early on that he was worthy of receiving Peter's time and attention. In other words, Bob had to be humble enough to know he needed a mentor, and he had to be aggressive and persistent enough to convince Peter to spend quality time with him. Additionally, Bob had to be committed to spending his own time and money to connect consistently with a mentor who lived 1,200 miles away.

Bob, who is in his fifties, is also someone who gets the "under forty" part of the 40:40 Principle. He values the wisdom and fresh eyes of those younger than he. He routinely invests in and learns from a group of ten young leaders through a strategic initiative he calls Bob, Inc. He also proactively inserts himself in the midst of next-generation leaders to update his perspective on how twenty- and thirtysomethings view the world.

> ## CONNECTING TIP #8
> *Create your own personal top five list of people you'd love to connect with, your dream team. Don't be afraid to aim high! Mention your top five list to at least ten people you already know and one or more of them will know someone on your top five list and make an introduction.*

Mitch and Morrie

Tuesdays with Morrie became a blockbuster publishing success, selling over fifteen million copies. It was a simple story about a young man searching the world in hopes of finding a more meaningful life, and the wise, older man giving sound advice to help him make his way.

As the story goes, author Mitch Albom flipped on the TV one night to ABC's *Nightline* and saw his favorite college professor from twenty years ago, Morrie Schwartz, being interviewed. Sixteen years had passed since Mitch had graduated college, and he'd lost touch with his mentor. As he watched the show, he learned that Morrie was dying of amyotrophic lateral sclerosis (Lou Gehrig's disease). He called him, and they began meeting once a week. Their thought-provoking conversations became the basis for the best-selling book *Tuesdays with Morrie.*

While Morrie was Mitch Albom's best-known mentor, many people strongly influenced Mitch throughout his life. "All my books are about mentors," he says.

Maybe you've lost track of early mentors as you've made your way through life, and their insights have faded. Wouldn't you like to see those people again, ask the bigger questions that still haunt you, and receive wisdom for your busy life today the way you once did when you were younger?

So what did Morrie do for Mitch? In their Tuesday conversations, he emphasized that people should place a priority on caring and compassion instead of material possessions. Morrie asked him questions like "Have you found someone to share your heart with?" "Are you active in your community?" "Are you working to be as human as you can be?" Mitch spent time reflecting on his life, which was spent squeezing activity into every minute of every day in his job as a sportswriter in order to achieve his primary goal of career accomplishment. "I traded lots of dreams for a bigger paycheck, and I never even realized I was doing it. Morrie helped me reformulate success." Today he defines success this way: "Doing something you are passionate about and have the drive about, and achieving something that makes the world just a little bit better—not just for you but for others, too."[14]

Think about It

- Bono's teachers made an effort to develop meaningful, lasting relationships with students through conversations. Who are the young people within your realm of influence? Do they know you below the surface?

- Are you still in touch with any of your early mentors?

- Cancer puts life in perspective. How would you answer Morrie's questions to Mitch? (Have you found someone to share your passions? Are you active in your community? Are you working to be as human as you can be?)

---

[14]   *Success Magazine*, December 2008, page 62.

Chapter 9

Tap into These Relationship Resources

The only difference between where you are
right now, and where you'll be next year at this
same time, is the people you meet and the books
you read. —Charlie "Tremendous" Jones

So far, we've talked a lot about inviting wise people on both sides of the age of forty to serve as mentors in your life. Another way to look at this is to think of these advisors as *strategic relationship resources.*

Throughout my life, I have benefited from a combination of three primary strategic relationship resources, and I believe they can work powerfully for you too! In this chapter, I'll detail the structure I have developed around these resources, based on meeting and speaking with dozens of mentors and combining their habits and disciplines in ways that work for me.

Individual Mentors

As we've been discussing, this is where it all starts: in relationships with individual mentors—people with a proven track record of success and the wisdom to apply their passion and knowledge. These people may include (but aren't limited to) your spouse, siblings, children (both young and old), parents, extended relatives, physician, attorney, minister/priest, therapist, counselor, professional life coach, coworkers, and neighbors.

Usually I start out by inviting potential mentors to meet with me once. If things seem to click between us, I will invite them to become my mentor for a period of one year. I group my team into these "big seven" categories. Each one is designed to feed the specific areas of my life that are most important to me at any given time.

1. Financial freedom
2. Thinking big and vision
3. Purposeful career
4. Physical fitness
5. Spiritual health/personal growth
6. Healthy relationships
7. World-class parent

Your list will probably look different from mine, because the things that are most important to you may not be the same for me. But this gives you an idea of how you might structure your mentor relationships. Here is a simpler classification system you might like better, which I call the Four Fs:

1. **F**inances
2. **F**amily
3. **F**aith
4. **F**un

My specific request to mentors is that we meet at least twice during the upcoming year, either in person or over the phone. You can meet as often as monthly if you like, but this might not be feasible if you have more than a couple of advisors. I strive to have between five and seven mentors in my life at all times. We agree that I can contact them to schedule our meetings, during which time I can ask them questions related to their particular category of expertise.

Most of the people I invite to become my mentors are more than willing to do so. They are honored that I asked them and impressed that I am this strategic about my life. They may not admit it, but trust me, they are taking notes themselves about how they can do the same thing in their own worlds.

One interesting thing I've found is that although I may think someone is a person of wisdom, he or she doesn't always agree. Maybe people are just being humble, but often people don't know how wise they really are and how much they have to offer. When I ask a business owner to meet with me to talk about her experience running a company, and she says something like, "Well, I don't think I have succeeded enough to warrant a responsibility like that," I respond, "Well, then, would you be willing to meet and tell me about the things that have *not* worked for you and the lessons you've learned from these mistakes?" This almost always convinces the business owner to meet with me and at least talk about it. Think about this: how many people do you know who are interested in learning about the *mistakes* you have made?

The truth is that most people are a bit fearful of being found out. You may think someone you admire is an A+ person, yet he fears that if he meets with you, you might find out otherwise and downgrade him to a B-. When you bring up the fact that you want to hear about his failures—because, after all, we seem to learn more from failure than we do success—this takes some of the edge off the perceived grading.

Friendtors

What is a friendtor? A friendtor is a peer who offers mentoring type advice but who is still primarily a friend, a peer. You know they're a friendtor if they don't fit into any other categories. Personally, I have up to a dozen of these guys and gals in my life. I bet you do too, or you should. More than likely, you are a friendtor to them at times. They fit in between a casual friend and a mentor. They can be family members, neighbors, or work associates. You may see them regularly or randomly. This is not an official role but rather an unofficial one. A friendtor offers advice, encouragement, and challenge when you need it. If you join an affinity group of like-minded men and women, these could be categorized as friendtors. A friendtor offers insight and oversight without you even knowing it. That's the beauty of it. But you must be on the lookout for friendtors, or you may miss the sage advice, piercing corrections, and crisp compliments. I have seen this friendtor relationship used in the workplace very well at a company in New York City called Next Jump. They are called TPs, short for talking partners. Everyone at Next Jump is encouraged to have a talking partner. TPs meet one-on-one every weekday morning to review business and life. Think of all the times you want to talk to the boss but can't get the time, or you just need to vent or get someone else's opinion. The TP is there every day to fill in for that need, and it goes both ways. Often, people just need someone to listen to them. As my friend Casey Sanders says, "Everyone wants to talk, it's just there aren't enough people who want to listen."

Be on the lookout for these random and not so random individuals, and realize that you could be getting better as a result of them.

It has been said that our income level
and our life values are the sum average of
the five closest friends in our life.

If the above quote is true—and boy, it sure seems to be true nine times out of ten—we need to be very selective about who we invite into our inner circles, as well as whose invitations we accept.

Team of Mentors

Teams of mentors are groups of individual mentors. Often referred to as affinity groups, mentoring groups, or personal boards of directors and advisory boards, they should generally consist of three to fifteen people. Teams can be formal or informal, but the most important success factors are that they consist of *wise people* and meet regularly and consistently. The American anthropologist Margaret Mead thoughtfully pointed out the power of this concept: "A small group of thoughtful people could change the world. Indeed, it's the only thing that ever has."

I maintain four of these kinds of teams in my life at all times, and I suggest that you have at least one. My first team is a board of directors for my nonprofit organization—ten men and women who offer feedback, ideas, and challenges around our mission statement. My second team consists of men only (gender-specific group), and our focus is to serve as each other's personal board of directors, band of brothers, advocates, and accountability partners. We talk more often than this and may even get together more often, but we formally meet for a half day each month to review personal and professional goals in a strictly confidential setting. Note that this is a high-trust group; anything and everything can be talked about— and usually is.

The third team is what I call a give-back group. Right now, my wife and I are leading a mentoring group of five newly married couples. What Nikki and I would have given to be part of such a group when we were first married! It's great to witness how the time we invest with these couples helps strengthen their marriages right before our eyes.

Finally, my fourth and most important team is my family: my wife, Nikki, and our three children, Drew, Cole, and Mati. I continually ask myself if I'm being intentional, available, and present with my wife and each of our kids, and if we are building enough photo album or Instagram moments together.

CONNECTING TIP #9
Make your family relationships your number one priority. Positive memories can never be erased. An epic family vacation cannot be taken away-it's in the bank.

It's important to note that family is the one team that always stays at the top of my list. Friends are a nice addition to my life, and church is a tool that supports family. But my wife and kids are the number one team that I've been called to lead, and it's the one that will outweigh everything else in importance when I'm lying on my deathbed.

Virtual Mentors

Finally, you should take advantage of what I call virtual mentors. These are personal relationship resources you can tap into at any time—tools like books, podcasts, Netflix documentaries, healthy TV programming, and commentaries. These are designed to *supplement* your connections with people, not replace them. Everyone has their own basic requirements and special needs, so ultimately you should determine what tools work best for you.

At a minimum, I recommend completing at least one book, podcast, or workshop a year on *each* of the following topics.

- *Relationships*—Communication and boundaries are popular topics.

- *Leadership*—Perhaps as a spouse, partner, parent, or in your career.

- *Physical health*—If you aren't healthy, most other things will no longer matter.

- *Career growth or financial management*—Professional growth and guidance on wise saving and investing.

- *Spiritual or personal growth*—Whatever is inspirational for you.

- *Motivation*—Anything that encourages positive thinking.

I recommend applying these basic tools to any topic that is urgent or critical in your life right now, whether at work or at home. Here are a few examples.

- Dealing with a career transition

- How to get promoted at work

- Starting or growing a business

- Personal or business financial management
- Preventing a divorce
- Dealing with depression or anxiety
- Parenting a blended family

Going Deeper

If you're interested in going deeper, there are a couple of advanced relationship tools that can help you get to the next level. These are my favorites, because most people don't have the vision or courage to attempt them, yet they hold the greatest potential for personal and professional growth for those who challenge themselves.

The first is what I call taking a personal retreat day. When was the last time you set aside a full day to be alone—I mean *all alone?*

When I was thirty-five years old, I invited a man named Barry Greco to be a spiritual mentor to me. He was Catholic and I was Protestant, and although most people would see this as an unusual connection, I looked at it as an opportunity to learn something new from someone with different traditions. True to form, that is exactly what happened, and I learned the retreat day concept in the process. Here's how it played out.

One day I asked Barry to suggest how I could get to the next level of personal spiritual growth. He looked at me to gauge my level of seriousness and then offered what I thought was a pretty bizarre suggestion. "I want you to take a day away from your office and the big city and do absolutely nothing."

Are you kidding? I thought. *Why would anyone waste a whole day doing absolutely nothing? Why would I not instead invest it in being highly productive?* My whole life up to that point had been one big, turbocharged productivity fest. Sitting there, I processed it a little more and decided that Barry must be playing some kind of psychological mind game with me—maybe even setting a trap to see if I would fall for it. I said, "Thanks, but no thanks. I'm not about to waste a whole day doing nothing."

His comeback was classic. "Okay, I have another idea. I want you to waste *two* days doing absolutely nothing!" He was dead serious.

I finally gave in, and later that month, I ventured off into the North Georgia mountains all by myself. Three significant memories come to mind as I think about that maiden voyage twelve years ago. The first was how odd it was to tell my wife. Picture me telling her, "Honey, I'm leaving for two days, to, um, just, well, you know, I'm going to go hang out in a cabin by myself." At first she was a little shocked, but she soon understood (as I had slowly also come to understand) the wisdom behind taking dedicated time away from the hustle and bustle of everyday life to think, dream, plan, and enjoy being alive, with the potential of coming back more refreshed, energized, and ready to tackle whatever lies ahead.

The second is my cigar man story. It was wintertime, and as I was driving up Blood Mountain at dusk, with the whole area covered by snow, I saw this guy with a big smile on his face and a cigar hanging out of his mouth. He was relaxed, at peace, and enjoying himself—or at least, that's the sense I got from my drive-by vantage point. At that moment, it hit me: how long had it been since I had done something just for me? Not in a self-indulgent way, but in a healthy way. How long had I been giving and giving to others? I had not taken time for myself. I reflected on summer days long ago as a young boy, when time to play, think, and dream was plentiful and normal. This was a time to reel in some of that energy.

The third memory from that retreat is the anxiety I felt as I first settled into my cabin in Vogel State Park with my stash of firewood, food, and reading material. Staring ahead at two full days of silence all alone, my mind began to wander, so I went for a run. This solved the problem for a few hours, but the anxiety soon returned. I decided to eat, which helped for another hour. Then I made a fire, read a book, and took a walk, but I was still anxious.

I remembered that Barry had said this would happen. When you are hardwired to work and work and work, you generally have two speeds: a hundred miles an hour, and neutral. He said the first day would be spent detoxifying from the frantic pace I had maintained over the years.

True to his word, I wrestled through day one with some enjoyment but plenty of anxiety. But by the time I'd finished breakfast the next morning, I had calmed down considerably. The sky was bluer than normal, and my head was clearer than I it had been in some time. I couldn't explain it, but the first thing I did was put a date on the calendar to do it again the next month. I sensed it would be nearly impossible to maintain a regular routine of this, so I wanted to get one more of these retreats in before it became a distant memory.

Why don't more people carve out time to get away and intentionally unplug like this? Every time I take somebody else on a personal retreat day—and I have been on more than seventy-five retreat days like this—life-changing things happen.

The best example is a retreat day I went on with a real estate investor and friend of mine. For six months he'd been trying to close a critical deal, but it was stalled and pending collapse. The future of his business hung in the balance, so not surprisingly, he was frustrated and anxious. As his mentor, I invited him to spend a day with me at a cabin in the mountains. "Are you kidding?" he screamed. "I could miss the deal, or some other opportunity that might pop up if I'm not in the office." I insisted that this was important, and he finally gave in and agreed to come.

I didn't say this to him, but I did not think the deal was going to happen for him *unless* he went away on a retreat day like this. I believe that a supernatural event occurs when a person surrenders and trusts in something as counterintuitive as "wasting" a day away alone in a mountain cabin to think, meditate, and pray, instead of being busy and productive in his office.

My friend had the day of his life, repeating over and over (as we all do when we finally get away) that he needed to do this more often. All those problems he had back in the big city were put in perspective. But here's the best part. On the way home, as soon as we hit cell phone range, his phone rang—with confirmation of the deal he had been awaiting for six months! I promise that things like this routinely happen during personal retreats.

To shake things up a bit, take a mentor or even a team along with you on your retreat day. Focus the day on adventure, brainstorming, or resting and relaxing. I'm a big fan of the solo retreat, but I like injecting a copilot at least a few times a year. It is always amazing to me how much there is to talk about when you scamper off with someone else for a daylong adventure. There seems to be an unspoken excitement in the air when you anticipate twelve hours of fun and freedom. How cool is that?

Since my first retreat adventure in 1999, I have averaged one or more days away on retreat each month. Most of these days, I leave town at 6:00 a.m. and return home the same day in time for dinner. Where do I go? Early on, I told a friend what I was doing, and he said, "We have a cabin that is never used. I'll give you the keys." A lot of people have second homes like this, but unless you have the conversation or ask, you'll never know. The most common reaction I get is, "Sure, you can use it. I only wish I could go with you!" But you don't need a fancy cabin. You can get just as much out of a retreat day spent outside and enjoying the great outdoors.

The Power of Fasting

To get the most out of your personal retreat day, consider refraining from food, sugar, caffeine, and any other stimulants for the entire day. This discipline will allow you to gain focus and self-control. Think about it: are there any areas of your business or life that could benefit from more focus and self-control?

Ten Reasons to Fast

1. Enhanced mental clarity
2. Better physical health
3. Improved self-discipline
4. Greater confidence
5. A renewed apprciation for simple foods
6. New empathy for those without even basic foods
7. Increased spiritual vitality
8. Cleasing of the gastrointestinal (GI) tract
9. Time saved not preparing and eating meals
10. Adventure - simply trying something you have never done

In the final analysis, fasting is an acquired habit that can bring many benefits, especially when accompanied with a retreat day. The length of time people fast, and the different things they fast from, vary widely. I make it a goal to fast from food for twenty-four hours at a time at least twice a year. During this time, I will drink a fresh-squeezed juice and usually one cup of coffee during the day. My main motivations are self-discipline, saving time, and spiritual vitality. Yours may differ, so experiment and come up with a plan that is aggressive yet realistic. Note that if you ever decide to fast from food for longer than twenty-four hours, you should consult your physician first.

Now you have a few ideas for ways to connect with mentors and some tools to support these connections. For many people, it is still a stretch to carve time out for people, especially new people, in this way. It's a mental and emotional strain, as well as a calendar challenge. But I promise that it's well worth the time and energy you invest. The benefits you'll reap include stress reduction, financial clarity, relational vitality, spiritual vigor, physical refreshment, and career vision.

Think about It

- Regarding virtual mentors, make a list of one book, podcast, or seminar you could complete within a year for at least four of the following six topics: relationships, leadership, career growth or financial management, spiritual or personal growth, motivation, and physical health.

- A supernatural event occurs when a person "wastes" a day alone in a mountain cabin to think, dream, and contemplate instead of being busy and productive at the office. What is your reaction to this counterintuitive statement?

- I described the benefits of unplugging from technology and the rat race for a personal retreat day. When was the last time you set aside a full day to be alone in nature?

- In addition to a monthly or quarterly retreat day, strive for weekly goals, like spending thirty minutes in silence on your back porch, or taking a nature hike.

Chapter 10

Make It Happen—Now!

A journey of a thousand miles begins
with a single step. —Lao-tzu

Connecting with mentors is integral to reaching your goals and dreams. However, most people think they can't afford to invest the time and money involved in meeting consistently with mentors. Of course, my response is that you can't afford *not* to. But how do you pull it off? The truth is connecting with others is really quite intuitive; you do it all the time with friends, family, and coworkers. The 40:40 Principle adds purpose and structure to what you are already doing and encourages you to be more strategic, creative, and aggressive in your efforts.

The first step is to commit *today* to taking the plunge. Make a decision to invite at least one mentor who is older than you and one who is younger than you to meet for coffee, breakfast, or lunch, or simply have a telephone meeting. If you already have mentors in your life, take this opportunity to reexamine and change them if necessary. Your ultimate success depends on it.

Your goal should be to bring between four and six mentors into your life, and ideally they can help in areas where you need the most support or need to be challenged. The primary types of mentors I've identified include the following.

Core Advisors (Essential)

- *Family*—A man or women with a great marriage, a person who has raised great children, or a certified relationship expert. Family may be your most powerful source of strategic advice.

- *Spiritual*—A pastor, volunteer church leader, or other person who can help nurture your spiritual growth

- *Physical*—Your primary care physician or a medical specialist.

- *Financial*—A professional financial advisor, such as a certified financial planner (CFP) or a certified public accountant (CPA).

- *Career*—A professional career counselor or coach who can advise you objectively in this area

Non-Core Advisors (Helpful)

- *Life skills*—A life coach or mentor.

- *Emotional and mental health*—A therapist, psychiatrist, or psychologist.

- *Special marriage and/or parenting*—Friends or professional counselors who can assist with blended families, for example.

- *Fitness*—A workout accountability partner, personal trainer, or nutritionist.

- *Legal*—An attorney who knows you and your family, and whom you can call if a legal need arises.

> ## CONNECTING TIP #10
> *Get started! Take the first step toward making connections now, and you'll start to feel a little momentum building. Nothing motivates like results.*

Addition by Subtraction

If you think you already have too many people and relationships in your life, start with some addition by subtraction: remove two or three people from your inner circle of associates. I'm talking about the kind of people who add little or no value to your life—or worse, toxic people who drain and exhaust you. I know this may sound harsh, and I'm not suggesting you remove all of these people from your life, just the ones who consistently overload you and drag you down.

Everyone has a few high-maintenance people in his life. Your job is to figure out how many you can effectively handle before they start bringing you down with them. In my experience, the maximum seems to be two high-maintenance people per family; any more than this, and these people's negative influences can potentially have a serious impact on those trying to help them.

How can you identify these kinds of people? They are unwise individuals who cannot or do not rightly apply information, who have a hard time making decisions, and who are often consumed by fear. Begin the process now of transitioning away from them and toward wisdom people. It may be difficult at first, but I promise you it will be well worth the effort.

As you make room for more wisdom people in your life, remember to keep it simple. You meet and interact with people every day, and this is no different. Make the call, send the e-mail, extend the invitation, and get started today!

Five Steps to Connecting One-to-One

Here is a simple, five-step process to help you navigate toward successful one-to-one connections and meetings with mentors. I have also created a more nimble revision to this list in Appendix II, "Seven Steps to Finding a Great Mentor." Both lists get you to the same end result, connecting one-to-one with a strategic advisor but you may prefer one list over the other.

1. *Create a list of candidates.* Start by writing down the names of your own personal top-ten—the ten people whom you would most like to become your mentors. Start big and work your way down, and don't hesitate to include heavy hitters on your list who you think might be out of your league. For some reason, it has always been easy for me to approach people like this. I've never worried much about whether they'd say yes or no; instead, I just move on to the next candidate on my list. Sometimes opportunities arise to approach people again later and revisit conversations. The biggest barrier to approaching heavy hitters in this way is fear. But when you think about it, what is there to be afraid of? In the beginning, I was so naive that I walked into many situations and played the village idiot!

As you create your list, think about the concept of six degrees of separation, which states that we're all just six human connections away from virtually anyone else in the world. For example, let's say you wanted to meet with the governor of your state. More than likely, you are only six people away from an introduction. I was challenged to do this when I was in my twenties, and as a result, I have met with more than one hundred high-achievement champions in many areas of business and life.

In fact, I have stretched myself to meet with some people I would never have dreamed possible, but one or two phone calls later, they were often receptive and open to meeting with me in person, and my life is exceptionally more robust having taken the risk and the time to try to connect with them. My current top-five targets are a president of the United States, Simon Sinek, Brene Brown, Oprah Winfrey, Anthony Robbins, and Bono. I also keep another list of potential mentors who are local and more accessible, and I work the list through each year.

This concept of stretching yourself is not a new one. More than 150 years ago, the English poet Robert Browning said it this way: "Ah, but a man's reach should exceed his grasp, or what's a heaven for?"

One of my first mentor reaches was during college. As I noted earlier, I was captain of the rugby team at Kent State University, and in my first year as captain, we were about the worst team in the Rugby Union. One day a few of us decided we could continue to fumble around during practices and matches, or we could go get help. I decided to take action. I asked around if there was anyone on campus with some serious rugby experience, and one name kept coming back to me: a professor named Patrick Brennan. I scheduled an appointment to meet with him and shared our story: we weren't very good, but we were committed to working hard, getting better, and ultimately winning a state championship. He became our faculty advisor and coach, and he taught us how to play real rugby, not the distorted form of American football we'd been playing. The following season we improved to a winning record, and the season after that, we were state champs. It pays to ask!

I suggest that you create a dream team list of at least five people for whom it would be a stretch for you to connect with, as well as another list of five to ten people who are more accessible. Work on compiling their contact information now so they're easier to reach once you get started. When creating your list of candidates, remember that you aren't looking for people who will pamper you. Instead, you want mentors who will tell you the hard truths and help you sort out confusion and overcome challenges. If you already have a stable full of these types of advisors, you might want to consider adding a "soft touch" advisor or two. But generally speaking, most of us need thoroughbreds who will challenge, encourage, and correct us, not yes-men who tell us what we want to hear.

2. *Define your reason for the connection and meeting.* Before inviting a candidate to meet with you, make sure you clearly explain to him or her the *specific* reason for the meeting. This will not only help

you clarify exactly what it is that you want to accomplish—business advice, vision casting, improved physical fitness, deeper spirituality, and so forth—but it will also help your potential mentor be better prepared to meet with you.

Clearly communicate this goal to your potential mentor before the initial meeting. It can be extremely awkward for someone to perceive that the purpose of the meeting is to offer you career advice, only to have it go in the direction of you asking him or her for a job. Make your intentions clear upfront and stick to them once the meeting starts. Remember, most people love to give advice and will often meet with you to offer their opinions and counsel.

3. *Make the invitations.* Send e-mails, make phone calls, approach candidates in person, or do all three. Your invitations should be clear and concise, explaining exactly what you're asking for (to meet one-on-one or to join a team or advisory board). Don't try to push or guilt someone into meeting with you. If a candidate seems lukewarm, move on to others. You want motivated, excited people on your team. Keep going until you have scheduled meetings with one or more potential mentors.

4. *Confirm the meeting.* Do so within five days of your scheduled meeting date with a quick e-mail, text, or Outlook meeting notice confirming the date, time, place, and topic for discussion. Successful people are usually busy people, and they appreciate these kinds of reminders and confirmations.

5. *Conduct the meeting.* Your initial meeting should consist of three phases. First, start off by restating the reason you are meeting and asking how much time the mentor has to meet. This will help put your potential mentor at ease and confirm what you have planned. The bottom line is to build trust with other strategic people, and taking these initial steps will do just that.

Second, get the ball rolling by asking some great questions. Most people are dying for others to be truly interested in them for *who* they are rather than *what* they do. Asking others to offer strategic advice is showing interest *in* them. Asking them to hire you, buy your product, or support your cause is attempting to get something *from* them. Do you see the difference? Show interest in the potential mentor and his or her wisdom, and then let the rest develop. These conversations generally take on a life of their own. See Appendix IV for a short list of powerful questions, and visit andychristiansen.com for an advanced list.

Third, conclude the meeting by communicating two or three specific things you gleaned from your time together. Also, be sure to respect your potential mentor's time by ending the meeting on time.

Be content with this initial meeting and don't expect anything more. If you desire another meeting, send up a trial balloon by saying something like, "This really helped me. I'd love to do it again!" If there is a favorable response, say you'll be in contact again in a few weeks to get something on the books for the next month or so. If he or she doesn't respond favorably, it may not mean anything. Either be content with your one meeting, or make contact again in a few weeks to see if the potential mentor is receptive to a future meeting. If not, you can always move on to the next person on your candidate list.

Here are two more critical points.

- *Always pay.* If meeting for coffee or a meal, be sure to pay the tab yourself. Not only is this proper etiquette, it is also respectful of and thankful for the potential mentor's time and knowledge.

- *Always say a thank-you.* Express sincere appreciation, and never overextend someone's time, interest, or energy. Afterward, send a *handwritten* note of thanks. Contrary to popular belief, these never went out of style and probably never will. An e-mail thanks is fine, but this should be in addition to a handwritten note.

Finally, think about what you would like this relationship to look like on an ongoing basis. Ideally, your initial meeting will grow into regular meetings, usually weekly or monthly. If so, structure your mentor meetings around topics or areas that are of particular interest or relevance to your life right now. For example, you could read a book or watch a DVD series together on such topics as business, personal finance, marriage, parenting, or personal growth. The important thing is to clarify each other's expectations up front. What are your main motives for meeting together on an ongoing basis? Agree on the frequency, length, and focus for each meeting. Most mentor relationships sour as a result of differing expectations.

Forming Mentor Teams

The simplest mentor relationship is a one-to-one connection. However, a team mentor environment offers some significant advantages over the one-to-one format, including the ability to:

- Gain wisdom from multiple sources rather than just one

- Obtain various viewpoints and perspectives other than your own

- Build a network of associates

- Experience camaraderie, brotherhood, or sisterhood

- Build confidence from having your point of view received by the team

I have seen marriages rescued and businesses revived as individuals tapped into the collective wisdom of a group to help them meet their unique challenges and receive wisdom they would probably not have acquired outside of a team environment.

As you consider forming a team of mentors or upgrading your current team, remember that people need and desire *purpose* in their lives. Don't believe me? Well, *The Purpose Driven Life* by Rick Warren is the best-selling nonfiction hardcover book of all time, with more than thirty million copies in print. Therefore, I suggest you seek out people who know where they are going in life. Purposeful people are usually successful, enthusiastic, and intelligent, and this rubs off on everyone around them. Keep your team focused on a clear goal or objective that is purposeful.

Just to be clear, I'm defining a team as a gathering of three to fifteen people. It can be formal or informal. The most common types of mentor teams are:

- *Affinity:* These are formed and bonded through a common interest or identification. Business roundtables, community volunteers, religious or spiritual small groups, and book clubs are a few examples of affinity teams.

- *Oversight:* These are usually found in the marketplace, like a board of directors. There is also a growing trend toward individuals forming personal boards of directors or portfolios of advisors.

- *Mentoring:* These are focused on imparting wisdom or specific knowledge upon younger or less experienced participants with a specific need.

I've found that one of the greatest hindrances to forming a team is fear. "What if everybody I ask says no? What if nobody likes each other? What if nobody shows up for the first meeting? What if people expect to be paid for their time?" In my experience, the latter is pretty much a nonissue, because most people chose to be mentors for the personal gratification they receive and do not expect to be paid. According to entrepreneur David Hersh of Jive Software in Portland, Oregon, who built a personal oversight board, "It's human nature to give advice. The people on my board do it more for ego gratification than anything else."

The steps to forming and connecting with a team are similar to those detailed previously for connecting with individual mentors, with a few twists.

1. *Define the purpose of the team.* Are you forming a team so everyone can share business advice, support a cause, challenge each other to set and achieve goals, or help each other grow spiritually? I suggest you define this clearly and put it in writing.

2. *Identify potential team members.* Who are the top ten to twenty people you would like to invite onto your team? As we discussed previously, stretch yourself by identifying some people you might think are out of your league.

3. *Identify a key ally.* Who can you ask to partner with you to champion your cause and help put this team together? For a personal board of directors, make sure this is someone who truly cares about you as a person. If you are building a business board of directors, identify this key ally before inviting anyone else. Go ahead and appoint him or her as your chairperson, if you can. If your chairperson has to be elected by the rest of the board, at least you'll know your top player.

4. *Make the invitations and send confirmations.* Similar to your preparation for meetings with individual mentors, send e-mails, make phone calls, approach candidates in person, or do all three. Confirm your meeting in a timely manner. Your invitations should clearly and concisely explain your expectations.

5. *Conduct the meeting and follow up promptly.* Like your individual mentor meetings, your group meetings should also consist of three phases: restate the reason for meeting, ask great questions and deliver prepared content, and recap the specific things you learned from your time together. As you wrap up, clearly communicate next steps and each person's assignments and to-dos. After the meeting, follow up via e-mail with a written recap and the date, time, and place for your next meeting, if there is to be one.

Keep It Simple

We often make all of this too complicated or sophisticated, so keep these three guiding principles in mind as you build your mentor team.

- *Get clear.* Make sure everyone on the team is crystal clear as to the need, vision, and reason for the team's existence. For example, in 2007 I formed an affinity group called 100X. The common vision and reason we meet together is to encourage and challenge each other to strive for 100 percent (100X) return on investment in this lifetime, whether in business, in the community, or within our families.

- *Get free.* Remove barriers that stand in the way of achieving your goals with this team. This might mean canceling appointments and saying no to projects if you have to, as well as overcoming limiting beliefs in yourself. If you can't identify what these barriers are for you, ask the people you're closest to; they know what they are.

- *Get going.* Finally, make your decision to act—and go for it! Remember, not everything you try will work, and this is especially true when it comes to groups and teams. After your first meeting, keep the things that worked and build on them. Throw out everything else.

Teams are powerful, but they take triple the effort to form and maintain as opposed to one-to-one mentor relationships. Think through all of these issues ahead of time, and use these guidelines to help form the basis of your unique team. Give yourself some freedom, and don't worry if you don't know exactly what the process should look like. It's a laboratory!

The Personality of Your Team

The most successful teams have the right mix of personalities. The wrong mix will hinder communication and inhibit honesty and openness. As you seek to put together a team of different personalities that will gel, try to include:

- A wide range of ages—ideally, at least one person who is both ten years older and younger than you

- Someone both riskier and more conservative than you

- At least one visionary or big thinker

- Someone who is a big fan of yours, and someone you know will tell it to you like it is

- A driven, "get it done" person
- An influential and inspiring person
- A quiet and supportive person
- A reserved, behind-the-scenes person

For an oversight group, choose members based on age and stage of life, gender (or mixed gender), and areas of expertise (financial, marketing, operations, etc.). For an affinity group, you will do well to keep the focus narrow—for example, spiritual growth, business development, marriage enhancement, or physical fitness—and include members of the same gender who are similar in age and stage of life.

Think about It

- Are there any toxic people currently in your life? Limit interaction with those who overload and drain you.

- Consider your greatest needs, and think about whom you know with proven success in those areas. Create a list of potential mentors that you could invite to serve on an individual or team basis.

- Make a decision today to take the plunge. Invite at least one mentor who is older than you to meet for coffee, a meal, or a telephone meeting.

- Extend an invitation to meet with a younger mentor.

Chapter 11

The 40:40 Payoff

At times our own light goes out and is rekindled by
a spark from another person. Each of us has cause
to think with deep gratitude of those who have
lighted the flame within us. —Albert Schweitzer

At this point, you may be asking yourself, "Is this 40:40 stuff really worthwhile? Andy, let's get to the bottom line: what will be the *payoff* for me if I do this?"

I'm glad you asked! I believe the greatest benefit you will realize from the 40:40 Principle is the ability to routinely and quickly make *wise choices*. This single concept will dramatically enhance your success in every area of life.

Think about all of the demands on our time in the twenty-first century, and how much this challenges your ability to be productive. For example:

- How many e-mails do you currently have in your inbox waiting for a response?

- How many text messages, Facebook friend invitations, Twitter tweets, and LinkedIn pings demand your time?

- How many phone messages are waiting for you?

- How many meetings do you need to hold but don't have time for?

- How many items are on your to-do list that you know can't be done today, this week, or this year?

Have you noticed the popularity of top-ten lists? Personally, I love them! They give me advice on things I'm interested in, and then I can decide whether I want to accept this top ten or go build my own. The problem, however, is we are so busy that we need someone else to do the hard work for us so we can make quicker, more knowledgeable decisions, whether it's about a new restaurant, HDTVs, household appliances, or something more important.

Every year, decisions in life become more and more critical. In this information age, we have more decisions to make than ever before. It doesn't look like the pressure will let up anytime soon, either. Do you have a system or a process in place for making wise choices in a timely manner, so they don't pile up and turn into urgent matters that are much more complicated and difficult to fix?

As I stated earlier and in Appendix I, everyone must define success. Write the following statement on a sheet of paper, filling in the blank, and keep it in front of you for ninety days.

"If I knew I could not fail, I would …"

Your answer will show what you truly value or the deep-seated passion planted inside of you. In essence, it will be *your* definition of success, different from anyone else's, and for good reason: we are *all* different.

Over the course of history, wisdom is the one constant benchmark of success. Ask yourself if you are gaining enough wisdom to be successful in life. Notice that I did not ask whether you are getting enough *information*, but whether you are getting enough practical wisdom to consistently make wise choices.

No Excuses!

Not surprisingly, the most frequent response I get from people who aren't connected relationally and aren't willing to put the 40:40

Principle to work in their lives is that they "don't have time." As you near the end of this book, this might be exactly what you're thinking, or maybe it's something else:

Objection #1: "I don't have enough time."

My response: We all have the same amount of time at our disposal: 24 hours each day, 168 hours each week, 8,736 hours each year. What you do with your time is up to you. Scrutinize how you currently spend your time, and ask yourself if these activities will help you get to where you want to go in life. If they aren't helping, then *make* the time to invite mentors into your life and put the 40:40 Principle into practice.

Objection #2: "I don't know enough people."

My response: Do you know at least one other person? If so, then you qualify. Just meet with *someone* in order to get started. He or she might point your toward someone else who could be your ideal mentor. Also, you can meet new people any day of the week. For example, visit a coffee shop, attend a party, or join a networking group. I have met some of the greatest people in these environments.

Objection #3: "I don't know the right people."

My response: Are you sure about this? Start by defining who the "right person" is to be your mentor. My prediction is that you will come up with at least three people you could contact within the next week about being your mentor, and at least one of them will be receptive. Go ahead—I challenge you to prove me wrong on this!

Objection #4: "I don't see the personal or professional value in it."

My response: Over time, most of us get used to doing things our own way. However, this limits us to our own wisdom and ability. Tapping into the power of others can multiply your capacities exponentially, whether in your personal or professional life.

Objection #5: "Other people will say no when I ask them to be my mentor."

My response: It's human nature to fear rejection; we all do to some extent. But I learned a long time ago that no is a tiny little word—two letters, to be exact—so why be afraid if it? Give equal weight to another two-letter word: go! If one person says no, then *go* on to the next person on your list.

Objection #6: "I don't feel worthy of someone else investing in my life."

My response: It's also human nature to feel unworthy at times. However, every human being is worthy of having another person invested in his or her life. If you really struggle with feelings of unworthiness, look for someone whose life you can pour *yourself* into first.

Objection #7: "When I do connect with other people, they won't like me when they really get to know me."

My response: This is another perfectly natural fear for most people. We all know what we're really like deep down inside— the parts of us that nobody else sees—and we're afraid others will discover that we're not all that great after all if we let them get too close to us. My advice? Get over it. Our greatest growth usually comes when we allow others to see the real us, warts and all, and then start improving the areas where we need the most work.

Objection #8: "I'd rather connect with other people via Facebook, Instagram, e-mail, or text messaging."

My response: This objection has become especially common the past few years, as social media has really taken off. Although these modes of communication have their place, they will never replace real face-to-face human connections and touch. This is what human beings were made for, and if we don't get enough of it, we will suffer in the long run.

Objection #9: "I can't learn anything from someone that much younger than me."

My response: As I noted earlier in the book, the idea of learning something of value from someone younger than you may be counterintuitive, but it's not illogical. Whether it's learning more about the latest technology or trends, or just soaking up the energy, optimism, and enthusiasm emitted by most young people, you have much to gain by connecting strategically with members of the younger generation.

Objection #10: "I can't learn from someone that much older than me."

My response: What do you really mean by this? Do you mean you can't relate to people older than you, or you're afraid they can't relate to you? Are you afraid they don't have a clue about the world you live in? Well, there's really only one way to find out, isn't there? The fact is those older than us usually have a wealth of life experience that can help younger people avoid many of the mistakes they've made in their lives.

Over the past twenty-five years, I have talked with hundreds of people about the 40:40 Principle. During this time, I've heard every excuse under the sun for why people can't or won't put the 40:40 Principle to work in their lives. But after much observation, I've concluded that when people say they don't have time or any other reason to be intentional about strategic relationships, it's because they have yet to discover how life-changing these relationships can be. People make time for what they think is important, so I believe it has more to do with *priorities* than with actual time.

Think about it: everybody spends time and money meeting with other people. The problem is that most of us aren't being *strategic* about whom we meet with, how we meet with them, and how often.

For example, how many lunches do you have every month with the boys, or how many nights out with the girls? You know, those friends of yours who talk about the same things every time you get together. I know there is a certain level of comfort and camaraderie in these relationships, and I enjoy them myself. But how many times a month do you need to cover the same ground with the same people? Or, how many hours do you spend with counterfeit relationships online or on TV? Instead, why not plan two or three coffees, lunches, or dinners each month with mentors? Choose a few who are older than you and more advanced in their profession or stage of life, and a few who are younger than you and whom you can ask about up-and-coming trends and their perspective on the changing world. We all need people ahead of us who can share their life experiences, as well as people in the more formative stages of life with fresh eyes and a fresh perspective.

Pay It Forward

In this book, we have focused primarily on how *you* can glean wisdom from mentors to live a fuller and more successful life. Now I'd like to turn the tables a little by suggesting that you think about what it might look like if you were to pay it forward by becoming a mentor for someone else.

I believe everyone has something to offer, and one of the best ways for you to give back is to serve as a mentor. I want to ask you to take the FOBO challenge: Find One, Be One! That's right, find a mentor and then be a mentor. See Appendix III for a simple outline. When we give and serve, our bodies releases a chemical called dopamine, which is the base of the English slang word for drugs—dope! Dopamine has an amazing effect on the human body; it gives us a euphoric feeling similar to a sugar or caffeine buzz. It's the rush you feel when you get a raise or promotion, land a big new client, or win a championship game.

Serving as a mentor for someone else is invigorating and energizing. In a world where we find ourselves so often on the defensive, it's empowering to take initiative in this way. So, after you've conducted a few dozen one-to-one meetings of your own and built your own team of mentors, challenge yourself to reach out and pour your life into at least one other person or group.

You might be wondering how this process works in reverse. In other words, if you desire to be a mentor for another person, should you actively seek out and approach people, or wait for them to ask you? After all, it can be a little awkward to walk up to someone and say, "Hey, it looks to me like you could use a little mentoring in your life. Would you like for me to be your mentor?"

This is a good question, and I think the best advice is to simply make yourself available. If you're like me and want to be intentional about it, you could start by forming an affinity or a mentoring group. For example, Nikki and I have started and facilitated dozens of affinity and mentoring groups. They all follow a fairly simple format: we find one other seed couple, with whom we decide on the focus and structure of the group and the types of people we think would benefit, and then we make a list of people to contact. We invite them to an initial meeting, where we share an overview and our vision for the group. If enough people are interested in joining, we start with a two-month trial run, after which time everyone decides if they want to keep going for six to twelve more months.

Becoming a mentor is one of the greatest gifts you can offer someone else. Much of my life has been influenced by my mentors—so much so that I frankly have no idea where I'd be today without them. It's all about pouring yourself into the lives of others, which is one of the healthiest things you can do. Here's an example from nature that helps illustrate this concept.

The Dead Sea, which is located in Jordan, is the lowest body of water on earth; it sits more than 1,300 feet below sea level. Ironically, although the Dead Sea is one of the richest bodies of water on earth, with the highest known concentrations of salt and minerals, it is also the *unhealthiest* body for actual habitation of fish and aquatic plants. Why is this? Because it has no outlet. There are no rivers or streams running into or out of the Dead Sea—it is literally stagnant.

Contrast this with the Sea of Galilee, which is also located in Jordan and sits about two hundred feet below sea level. The Sea of Galilee is one of the *healthiest* bodies of water in the world for the exact opposite reason. It is fed by the Jordan River from the north, as well as other lesser streams and underground springs, and the Jordan River continues to flow out of it to the south.

Now think of this in terms of human relationships. The Dead Sea is like a person who is always receiving, or being poured into, but never gives back or pours into others. Such a person will soon grow stagnant, just like the Dead Sea. Conversely, the Sea of Galilee is like a person into whom other people are pouring good things, and at the same time, he or she is pouring out good things into the lives of others.

Here are three things to keep in mind as you consider becoming a mentor.

1. *Be available.* As I said previously, when you are available, people will find you. Like usually attracts like, so be on the lookout for someone like you.

2. *Be selective.* Don't offer to be a mentor to just anyone. Be especially cautious of toxic people, which we talked about earlier, who will drain you mentally and emotionally. Instead, look for people with these qualities.

- Faithful—They will be willing to do the hard work that is often necessary in order to make real change happen in their lives.

- Available—They will make a commitment to being consistent and meeting with you when and where they say they're going to.

- Teachable—They will be open to constructive feedback and correction.

3. *Be the outcome you desire.* Values are caught more than they are taught. What you *do* will be much more important than what you say, so be sure to walk the walk and not just talk the talk. Also, be sure to schedule time together just to have fun—not every meeting or get-together has to be serious.

If you are not sure about this step, take it slowly. Most people say they don't want to make the commitment to being a mentor because they lack the time, money, or knowledge. However, you're only talking 60-90 minutes initially, very little money and no special knowledge if using the 40:40 principle.

So, complete the first meeting and then decide whether to move forward.

Think about It

- How would you rate yourself in the area of time management and productivity?

- Think you don't have time to invest in these relationships? Everybody spends time with people. The problem is that most of us aren't strategic about whom we meet with and how we meet with them.

- Which body of water best characterizes your life, the Sea of Galilee or the Dead Sea? What are your areas of expertise, and how could you pour into others?

Chapter 12

Do You Really Need This?

---

*Words mean much more than what is set down
on paper. It takes the human voice to infuse them
with deeper meaning. —Maya Angelou*

So, can you get what you want out of life without engaging
the 40:40 Principle? My grandfather, Claude A. Carr, didn't seem
to think so, and neither did his son Buck Carr. Neither did these
influential thinkers and writers.

"Most people have powerful connections. Very few people
have harnessed the power of their connections." —*Jeffrey
Gitomer*

"Refuse good advice and watch your plans fail; take good
counsel and watch them succeed."—*Solomon*

"Most of my focus on developing others focused on each
person's self-development. I have been wrong on this. The
potential rather was hiding within each relationship in my
life." —*Tom Rath*

"Today we are faced with the pre-eminent fact that if
civilization is to survive, we must cultivate the science of
human relationships." —*Franklin D. Roosevelt*

What does your gut tell you? Do you think you can achieve all your dreams and goals alone? And even if you can, will it be as rewarding? If you stand alone at the finish line, will it satisfy you?

Two Funerals

The following story helps to vividly illustrate the potential difference between a life lived primarily in relational isolation, and one that was relationally engaged and poured out into others.

A middle-aged man named Mark recently got a call informing him that his old boss, Jack Whitaker (not his real name), had died the day before. Jack's funeral would be held that upcoming Saturday. Jack Whitaker was a hard-charging, no-nonsense entrepreneur who didn't have time to build many relationships or make many friends during his life. He was only sixty-five years old, but Mark wasn't surprised he had died at such a relatively young age, given the way he had driven himself. Though he didn't really want to attend the funeral, Mark felt obligated out of respect for the man who'd employed him a number of years ago.

A few hours later, Mark received another unexpected call. This time, he was told that his close friend and mentor, Larry Sumner (not his real name), had just died, and his funeral would be on the same Saturday. This news hit Mark hard. Over the past two years, he had grown extremely close to Larry because they had met together for breakfast or coffee once a week, with Larry sharing his seventy years' worth of life experience and wisdom with Mark about everything from faith to family to career.

As the day of the funerals approached, Mark began thinking about each man's life and how different they were. Larry was a man of modest means who had a successful career in insurance sales but wasn't rich by anyone's definition. Meanwhile, Jack was extremely successful in business and had even donated large sums of money to many charitable causes, including the local hospital that named a new wing after him. But there were trade-offs, as his funeral was about to make painfully obvious.

Jack's funeral was first, at eleven o'clock on Saturday morning. The small suburban church was barely half full as the preacher gave the standard eulogy about life and death and how Jack seemed to have been taken too soon. He talked about all his business accomplishments and charitable gifts, and after he'd finished his remarks, Jack's wife spoke. She let everyone know that Jack had been a dutiful husband and father, providing well for her and their four children. Then the preacher gave a chance for others to come up and voice their respects for Jack. However, no one came forward—not a single person. The service wrapped up a little earlier than Mark had expected, which made it easier to get to Larry Sumner's funeral on time.

As Mark made his way downtown to his mentor's funeral, his mind raced with thoughts about both men. His former boss had required an inordinate amount of time and energy from Mark. At the time, Mark had accepted it as part of the job, but now he started to realize just how much he really resented those demands. But Larry Sumner had invested a tremendous amount of time and energy *into* Mark. As he reflected further, Mark realized that one of these men spent the majority of his life building a legacy in business by investing in his company and career, whereas the other man built a legacy investing in his business, family, and friends.

As he arrived at the church, Mark immediately noticed something very different from the first funeral, starting with the packed parking lot and long line of cars waiting to get in. He finally found a spot to park about a half mile away. Larry Sumner's funeral began much like the morning funeral. The preacher gave the typical eulogy, but this time to a standing room only crowd. After Larry's wife spoke tenderly of her husband, the preacher gave an opportunity for anyone else who would like to say a few words to approach the pulpit. Without even thinking about it, Mark found himself standing up and walking toward the front of the church to pay his respects to this man who, week after week and month after month, had poured himself into Mark, asking nothing in return. Dozens of others did the same. When it concluded, the event was less a funeral than it was a celebration of the life of a man who had touched the lives of hundreds of other people in profound ways.

As Mark drove away, the differences between the two men's funerals—and more important, their *lives*—hit him like a ton of bricks. Before Mark were two clear options for how he could invest his life: in the accumulation of money, possessions, and position, or in the lives of others. Which funeral did he want to be *his* on the day when he was laid to rest?

It's easy to read this story and think, *Of course, I want to be remembered after I'm gone for pouring my life into others and helping make the world a better place.* But is this what you're actually *doing*? Or have you let yourself get caught up in the never-ending, twenty-first-century rat race, constantly striving to earn more money and accumulate more possessions while neglecting the relationships that make life worth living? Decide what you want in this area today, and let mentoring with the 40:40 Principle make it a reality for you.

Make Mentoring with the 40:40 Principle Your Own

My grandfather lived an extraordinary life. He lettered in seven high school sports, went on to graduate from college with honors, married in storybook fashion, had three children, and ran a successful business. When he died at seventy-two years of age, hundreds of friends and family attended his funeral, which was a celebration of his life. Everyone spoke positive words, and my grandmother said she would never marry again because she could never find another man like my grandfather. She went on to live another twenty-six years, completely content as a widow. Claude A. Carr's legacy lives on through six grandchildren and twelve great-grandchildren.

What's going to be your legacy? Claude A. Carr summed up (via my Uncle Buck) what he thought the secret to a successful life was by stating one of the guiding principles of life for me: the 40:40 Principle. What will you do now that you have learned the secrets of this powerful principle? I challenge you to take ownership of mentoring with the 40:40 Principle; make it your own, and see where it takes you.

I'd love to hear how mentoring with the 40:40 Principle has helped you reach your goals and achieve more success. Please contact me at andy@capacity7.com with your stories.

Think about It

- Do you think you can achieve all your dreams and goals alone? And even if you can, will it be as rewarding?

- Remember that the greatest hindrance to forming strategic relationships is fear. Move past your fear and take a risk. Your success in life depends on it.

- Ponder the difference between the two funerals. What do you want others to say about you at your funeral? What will be your legacy?

Chapter 13

Workplace (Corporate) Mentoring Program

Put your staff first, customers second, and
shareholders third. —Sir Richard Branson,
founder and CEO of Virgin Group

I speak to a lot of CEOs and business owners groups, and one of my favorite questions to ask them is, "What's your biggest top of mind challenge right now?" You may think the answer would come back as investment capital, funding or a lack of time, but most often the response is a people problem. This begs the question: If people are the organizations biggest problem, why then does training and development get so little time and money compared to other business objectives? The average company spends more on annual office supplies than it does on developing employees. I heard this exchange between the CEO and CFO and thought it was very appropriate.

CFO: What happens if we train them and they leave?
CEO: What happens if we don't and they stay?

While I won't be diving deep into corporate mentoring in this book, I did want to introduce the topic and give you a resource where you can get more information and solutions. For more information on corporate mentoring programs and a free white paper on how to develop a successful corporate mentoring program, visit www.capacity7.com or www.the4040principle.com

Appendix Toolbox I

Define Success

Appendix Toolbox I

Define Success
Defining your vision of success

Webster's Dictionary defines success as "the achievement of something planned or attempted." Remember, your definition of success is neither right nor wrong, good nor bad; it is simply your vision of your ideal life.

In my opinion, what gets a lot people hung up is the overuse of motivational terms like goals, mission, vision, objectives, purpose, calling, etc. In one way or another, these terms all tie back to what it means to be successful.

Now take a stab at it by filling in the blank below. Fight the urge to make it perfect.

> *When you discover your mission, you will feel its demand. It will fill you with enthusiasm and a burning desire to get to work on it."* – W. Clement Stone

Success for me is:

_____

_____

_____

_____

_____

_____

_____

To download a printable version of this appendix or to see video content on this topic, visit www.the4040principle.com.

Appendix Toolbox II

Seven Steps to Finding a Great Mentor

1. **Decide**: Make a definite decision that you want a mentor, and be intentional in your pursuit of one.

2. **Aim High**: Don't settle for average. Success begets success, and failure begets failure. Go after what you want with enthusiasm.

If you reach for the ceiling, you won't
get off the ground, but if you reach for
the stars, you'll get to the ceiling.

---

3. **Focus**: Think deep, not wide. Too many people make the mistake of searching for an all-knowing sage or perfect mentor. There are no perfect mentors. Rather, use the list below to identify one of seven areas of familiarity, and then seek out people with experience or history there.

4. **Ask**: Build a list of five to ten candidates and start dialing, e-mailing, and texting, or ask in person. Don't worry about people saying no; it will happen, but most will say yes.

> "Discern the vital few from the trivial many." —Greg McKeown

> "Take risks now and do something bold. You won't regret it." —Elon Musk

5. **Press On**: When and if someone says no to your request, ask why. I have found that some people are insecure or overly humble. They don't think they know enough or have enough experience to add value. Let them know all you would like to do is hear their stories, and if all they can share are stories about things they did wrong, that's okay. Sometimes it's profitable to hear how people failed at things and then how they overcame.

6. **Meet Up**: Set up the meeting, confirm the meeting a few days in advance, honor the time you set by wrapping up on time, and always pay the bill if there is one. Keep your initial meeting light, ask about them, and listen twice as much as you talk.

7. **Thank Them**: Make sure you thank them in person, and follow up with a hand-written note to stand out!

    Areas of Familiarity

    1. Financial
    2. Thinking big
    3. Career
    4. Physical fitness and diet
    5. Spiritual and personal growth
    6. Relationships
    7. Parenting

Mentoring Networks

findamentor.com
score.com
thementoringproject.com
mentoringwomensnetwork.com
micromentoring.org
mentoring.org
passthetorchforwomen.com

Appendix Toolbox III

Mentors: Find One, Be One

THE [FOBO] MENTORING CHALLENGE

Find one, - Be one

Collaboration is one of the best kept secrets of creativity.
    – John Briggs
One of the best ways to love another person is to listen to them.
    – Unknown

The [FOBO] mentoring challenge says, find one person over 40 to meet with and if there's a good connection, meet again, and again. At the same time, intentionally reach out to someone younger and meet with them, and if there is a good connection, meet again, and again. Whether it's one time or multiple times you are gaining wisdom and getting better. Embrace it - repeat it - enjoy it. Do this for one year.

Find One:
Someone over 40 or 10 years your senior in age or experience:
Name   _____
Contact   info   _____
What questions do you want to ask them?_____
_____

Be One:
Someone 10 years your junior in age or experience:
Name _____
Contact info _____
What questions do you want to ask them?_____
_____

Everyone wants to be heard, but no one is listening.

    – Casey Sanders

To download a printable version of this appendix, visit www.the4040principle.com

Appendix Toolbox IV

Powerful Questions

Questions to Set up Active Listening

Create your own list of personalized questions. Make sure they are open-ended statements or questions that elicit information ("Tell me about the meeting"), as opposed to close-ended ("Did your meeting go well?"). Never ask questions that can be answered with yes or no, because they do not create dialogue. For more support on this topic, visit www.the4040principle.com.

Here are a few good, basic icebreaker questions.

1. What are your expectations for this meeting? For this event? For this next hour?

2. What is your greatest accomplishment in life?

3. What has been your greatest regret or failure?

4. If you could own any car, what would it be?

5. Tell me about ... Tell me *more* about ...

6. If you could live anywhere in the world, where would you live?

7. What are you most passionate about?

Advanced Questions

Here are a few more powerful questions after you get beyond the icebreakers.

- What is your greatest challenge right now (professionally or personally)?
- What do you love? What do you hate?
- What are you thinking about right now? What is topmost in your mind?
- What areas of life or work could you upgrade right now?
- What has made you smile lately?
- If you had ten million dollars in the bank, what would you do next?
- What are you crystal clear on right now?
- What do you really want out of life?

To kick it up a notch, after a few minutes say, "Tell me more," and wait for the other person to elaborate. Resist the temptation to fill the air; silence is golden here.

Follow-Up Questions (if you are managing or leading someone)

- If I could only do one thing to help you right now, what would it be?
- What can you learn from this?
- What are your top three strengths?
- On a scale of one to ten, how would you rate your performance at work? At home? What can you learn from this?
- What would you say is your vision for your company?
- From where you sit today, what would you say is your mission in life?

- If you had to answer the question you just asked me, how would you respond?

- What can I do to help you?

- What has been your greatest joy as a parent?

The next time you meet with this person, ask, "Hey how is that [event or project] going we talked about last time?" I call this inspecting what was expected. Offer praise when they hit the bull's-eye. What's rewarded gets repeated!

There is no substitute for a person who truly cares about another person. If you fake being interested, it's only a matter of time until you are found out. Be real—there is no greater thing to be!

To download a printable version of this appendix, visit www.the4040principle.com.

Appendix Toolbox V

Powerful Listening

When it comes to listening, you must strive to be *interested* rather than interesting. This will help create dialogue and trust rather than defensiveness. For more information on this topic, visit www.the4040principle.com

Types of Listening, Defined

Level I:
Passive listening focuses on what the conversation means to *me*.

Level II:
Active listening focuses on what's being said
and what it means to the *other person*.

Level III:
Superhuman (or Mach 1) listening includes reading body
language, emotions, tone of voice, and the environment.

What if you are not a great listener? Join the club, because most people aren't. Listening is like a muscle: the more your work it, the stronger it gets. Safeguard yourself by starting out with people who may take advantage of your listening ear. Say to them, "Hey, I'm not the best at listening, but I'm working on improving this skill. I have a five-minute attention span, so lay it on me." Then, after five minutes, ask them, "So, what do you think your next step will be to solve your top-of-mind issue?" Let them know when your five-minute listening span has expired. For the sake of not being rude, tell them you need to change subjects.

Remember: *The power of listening first lies in the power of the question.*

Frank B. "Buck" Carr

Contact Info:
Andy Christiansen, PCC, CLC
For Speaking or Consulting: andy@capacity7.com
Twitter: @achristiansen
Instagram @andy.christiansen
Book Web: the4040principle.com
Corporate Mentoring: capacity7.com